MILWAUKEE GHOSTS AND LEGENDS

MILWAUKEE GHOSTS AND LEGENDS

ANNA LARDINOIS

Haunted America

Published by Haunted America
A Division of The History Press
Charleston, SC
www.historypress.com

Cover image courtesy of Troy Freund Photography, 2017.

First published 2018

Manufactured in the United States

ISBN 9781467138178

Library of Congress Control Number: 2018942429

Notice: The information in this book is true and complete to the best of our knowledge. It is offered without guarantee on the part of the author or The History Press. The author and The History Press disclaim all liability in connection with the use of this book.

CONTENTS

Acknowledgements

No person accomplishes anything alone, and it is in that spirit I'd like to thank the following people and groups, without whom I could not have started on my spook-tacular journey.

WWBIC, whose contributions helped turn Gothic Milwaukee from a hobby into a vibrant member of the Milwaukee storytelling community.

My KIVA Zip investors, the generous people who believed in me before anyone else did—even myself. I am forever grateful to each of you.

The special support and patronage of the following very dear people: the Bonesteels, the Merbeths, the Nelson-Rowes, the QuAbbots and my posse members Angie, Caroline, Jackie, Jen, Jill and Wendy.

The Milwaukee County Historical Society, for being gracious hosts and very generous with its resources, and the Milwaukee Public Library, whose microfilm collection was a necessity in completing this project.

My acquisitions editor, John Rodrigue, whose incredible patience makes him a delight to work with.

Finally, a big thank-you to Corey Lardinois, whose support, encouragement and unfailing patience have made all things possible.

INTRODUCTION

No collection of Wisconsin-based ghost stories would be complete without a reference to celebrated folklorist Robert E. Gard's oft-repeated claim that Wisconsin has more ghosts per square mile than any other state. While his assertion is impossible to prove, there does seem to be something about Wisconsin that compels restless spirits to remain among the living. There is no part of the state that does not have its own haunted buildings, celebrated specters and eerie local legends. Milwaukee, Wisconsin's largest and one of its oldest cities, is rife with supernatural tales waiting to be discovered by the curious.

While we have yet to identify a way to definitively prove the existence of ghosts, every effort has been made to ensure the historical accuracy of the stories presented in the book. When names, dates or other factual evidence are presented, the information obtained is the result of academic research. Archived newspaper reports were the source of much of the material presented, as were the works of other well-known Wisconsin writers working in this genre. The writings of Linda S. Godfrey, Sherry Strub, Beth Scott and Michael Norman are required reading for anyone interested in Milwaukee's haunted history, and a debt of gratitude is owed to those authors and all others who have documented and preserved the city's oft-told ghostly tales.

A few well-known Milwaukee hauntings have been omitted from this collection in favor of lesser-known tales. A fan of the city's most famous ghost stories may be surprised to find tales from the Lady Elgin, Giddings Boardinghouse and other popular legends missing from these pages.

Traditionalists should be comforted to note that other notable stories, like Milwaukee's most famously haunted building and city's spookiest college campus, are included, along with tales from the past that might be now unknown to readers but are equally spine-tingling.

It is a true love of storytelling that brings me to collect stories of the supernatural. Long Wisconsin winters are perfect for snuggling up next to the fire and reading eerie tales of otherworldly events while the wind howls through barren tree branches, and I have spent many nights doing just that. From childhood, I have always loved stories, and as I aged, I grew to appreciate scary stories beyond the visceral reaction they cause. I discovered that ghost stories are a wonderful way to access the history of a city and to make the past come alive.

My interest in ghosts, stories and history has made me an avid fan of ghost tours. These tours quickly became my favorite way to explore new cities, and I still take a tour in each city I visit. My love of participating in ghost tours led me to develop my own walking ghost tour in Milwaukee in 2012. The tour has grown, and in 2016, *USA Today* named my tour, Gothic Milwaukee, one of the "10 Must-See Halloween Events in Wisconsin"; in 2017, *AAA Living* identified the tour in its listing of three of the best tours in the state. The most exciting distinction received has been being named by *Shepherd Express* readers as Best Milwaukee Tour in 2017, an honor that means a great deal because it came directly from those who have taken the tour. I am very proud of the tour and excited to be able to provide Milwaukee ghost story enthusiasts even more spooky stories from the Cream City.

THE SPOOKY SUBURBS

Milwaukee may have more than its share of ghosts, but that does not mean the surrounding areas do not have their own enduring haunts, legends and specters. No matter which road you take out of town, it is likely you are heading into a stretch of land with its own spine-tingling tales of the supernatural. Use this chapter as a starting place to begin to explore the spooky suburbs; for the cautiously sensible, it's a shortlist of towns to bypass on late-night drives alone. Sometimes the things that go bump in the night are best avoided.

THE DEADLIEST OF DEAD ENDS: FITZSIMMONS ROAD, OAK CREEK

Oak Creek's infamous "road to nowhere," Fitzsimmons Road, has been closed to traffic for more than twenty years, but that has not stopped visitors, both mortal and spectral, from visiting this eerie stretch of road.

In the 1950s and 1960s, this out-of-the-way, dead-end road was used as a drag racing strip by adventuresome local teens. A typical race night would find the popular strip lined with cheering crowds, illuminated only by the headlights of the reckless racers. Cars would tear down the strip, all revving engines and squealing tires, until the races abruptly concluded where the pavement stopped on the dead-end road…or so they should have. At the base of the road is a barricade alerting drivers to the end of the road, but

The notorious railroad crossing on Fitzsimmions Road. *Author's collection.*

the thin wooden barrier offered little resistance for the twenty tons of racing steel barreling down the deserted lane. Just beyond the barricade is a cliff that hovers two hundred feet above Lake Michigan. The eighteen-story drop into the water meant certain death for the unlucky racers. Legend has it that a number of racers, unable to stop at the barricades, careened off the jagged cliff and plunged to their watery graves at the bottom of the lake.

These days, cars are no longer able to access this closed part of Fitzsimmons Road, yet late-night thrill-seekers are still drawn to the spot, eager to see for themselves the mysterious headlights racing down the road and beyond the barricades that reportedly haunt the strip. Ghost hunters, traveling on foot beyond the railroad tracks, claim to hear sounds of engines revving, sometimes joined by the sounds of cars crashing and terror-filled screams. A number of people have claimed to see the apparition of a young man, a glowing white figure in the darkness, scaling the cliff on his way to Fitzsimmons Road. These spirits that remain, pulled from life so unexpectedly, appear to be forever trapped on the tragic night of their final race. This deadly street continues to attract the curious living as well as the restless undead.

Hidden Haunchyville: Mystic Drive, Muskego

For generations, curious thrill-seekers have traveled down Mystic Drive in Muskego in search of Haunchyville. Legend has it that just beyond this dead-end road lies a secret community of dwarfs. This group of reclusive former circus performers created their own town, hidden from the world by forest and cornfields. Those looking for the community know to proceed with caution, as it is believed Haunchyville inhabitants are protected by a single, typical-sized man armed with a shotgun and no aversion to shooting trespassers.

Based on the stories surrounding the area, those looking for this hidden hamlet would much rather be found by the trigger-happy guard than the bloodthirsty residents of the mysterious community. Whispered warnings are made to those who dare to seek the forbidden area. Frightening tales of the violence done to typical-sized people who disturb the seclusion of the Haunchyville residents are meant to keep explorers far from the dangers of the area. Some claim that "Haunchies" have enacted revenge on trespassers by severing the offenders' legs at the knees. Still others tell a tale of a young couple walking through a cornfield suddenly surrounded by a silent gang of residents who were armed with exceptionally sharp and pointed small daggers. As one, the group emerged from the shadows to form a tight ring around the couple, stabbing the pair until their bloodied bodies lay lifeless on the ground. Despite these tales of danger, or perhaps because of them, Haunchyville continues to be a destination that intrigues the curious.

Mystic Drive has changed a great deal since these stories began. Cornfields have made way to sprawling suburban yards, and each year that passes finds the tangle of woods at the end of the road smaller than the last. As the land is cleared for new homes, it is harder to believe this secret community exists. Despite growing evidence, true believers won't be dissuaded in their certainty that Haunchyville is real. Online forums are filled with eyewitness accounts of those who claim to have seen a field of tiny, perfectly formed homes that were later destroyed when a modern subdivision was built on the site. In an effort to deter curious trespassers, a coded privacy gate was installed on Mystic Road, which was seen as proof that the hidden community was tantalizingly near. Even the police presence on the road is interpreted by believers of evidence of the secret community. The heavily patrolled road features a number of "No Trespassing" signs, and the patrolling officers have no qualms with issuing a $334.50 trespassing ticket to those looking for the rumored community.

Police claim that they are protecting the safety and privacy of the residents of Mystic Drive, while believers see it as more evidence of collusion between the Muskego police and residents of Haunchyville.

Does Haunchyville exist? It seems that even if it once did, it is unlikely to still be located at the end of Mystic Drive. Perhaps this is why new tales of Haunchyville have surfaced, with promises of finding the colony in South Milwaukee locations like Cudahy's Sheridan Park and in Grant Park, just beyond the storied Seven Bridges. Only time will tell if thrill-seekers will abandon the search on Mystic Drive and focus their efforts on these urban oases.

THE BRAY ROAD BEAST: BRAY ROAD, ELKHORN

On a lonely stretch of rural road in Elkhorn, Wisconsin, lurks a mysterious creature that has astonished all those who have seen it. Known as the Beast of Bray Road, there are dozens who have claimed to have encountered the being many believe to be a werewolf. While descriptions of the Beast vary in specifics, it is often described as a creature that stands on two legs and is anywhere between five and seven feet tall. Reported as having a shaggy coat of long, dark hair, some witnesses have stated that the fur is streaked in silver or gray. While most have described the creature as having a head similar to that of a German Shepherd, with an elongated muzzle and pointed ears, a few claim that the Beast has a head that more closely resembles an ape than a dog. Although witnesses are not consistent on all aspects of the creature's appearance, there is one trait all who have encountered the Beast of Bray Road agree on: the intense, penetrating stare from the animal's cold, yellow eyes shook them to their souls.

The first known sighting of the Beast was in 1936 by a nighttime security guard at St. Coletta's, a home for the developmentally disabled. The rural, isolated campus is best known for its most famous resident, Rosemary Kennedy, who, as the result of a failed lobotomy, was confined to the institution from 1941 until her death in 2005. While patrolling the grounds after midnight, the watchman encountered a creature clawing the ground. As the man approached, the animal advanced toward him, rising from its haunches to reveal an erect height of more than six feet. The stunned man said that the animal was covered in dark hair and smelled strongly of putrid flesh. The creature stared into the eyes of the man, holding his gaze steadily as it sounded a deep, unearthly growl. The terrified guard quietly crept away, feeling the heat of the beast's eyes boring into his back while he prayed the animal would leave him unharmed.

Unscathed yet shaken, the frightened man never again encountered the beast, but many others have. A rash of unexplained sightings in the late 1980s and early 1990s led Elkhorn writer Linda Godfrey to cover the sightings in the local newspaper, *The Week*. Spotted prowling around Bray Road, a single-lane rural road surrounded by farmland, the creature became associated with this dark stretch of sparsely populated road. It is these encounters that gave the creature its current moniker. Those who saw the animal were struck by its human characteristics and panther-like run as it fled from the unexpected human encounters. The notable claws of the animal are said to have dug into a number of cars whose drivers encountered the Beast. There are a few who are so unnerved from their experience with the animal that they are convinced it has some occult connections.

Far from solving the mystery, the release of the articles detailing the sightings of the Beast of Bray Road brought more reported sightings and even national media attention. Despite the best efforts of those who wished to discount the sightings, no credible evidence has ever proven that the creature seen by witnesses was a wolf, bear, stray dog or any other known animal.

A Road Not Aptly Named: Paradise Road, Jefferson

The power of an urban legend can be surprisingly strong. The draw of Paradise Road in Jefferson is a testament to the power of storytelling and the human desire to be scared witless. A late-night trip to Paradise Road is a rite of passage for area teens, who have graduated from playing Ghost in the Graveyard and are now looking for their own ghosts.

Highly improbably stories are attached to the area, including versions of a story in which three witchcraft-practicing sisters were hanged in the woods. It may be this persistent story that has caused the widespread belief that the road is a hotbed of occult activity. Carloads of curious teens creep down the road, scanning for the robed figures who supposedly lurk in the woods. Graffiti depicting pentagrams and other symbols associated with Satanism can be found on road signs and the pavement itself, adding to the persistent belief that the Devil himself is present and found just feet from the road, beyond the tree line.

Does something sinister lurk in the idyllic woods just beyond Paradise Road? *Author's collection*.

Visitors to the remote, rural lane swear that a sinister energy surrounds this stretch of Paradise Road. Those brave enough to roll down the car windows as they pass are certain they hear screams from the woods. The screams are described as not quite human sounds but definitely bone-chilling. Those who dare to visit know their cars may not keep them safe; vehicles have been known to mysteriously malfunction on this eerie stretch of road, leaving terrified motorists trapped and vulnerable.

Perhaps there is something sinister in these woods. A murder did occur on this road, but it likely had nothing to do with the spirits of hanged witches or hooded figures practicing the black arts. In 1994, a teacher's aide at Jefferson High School convinced three students to aid her in the murder of her husband. The students did enter the Paradise Road home and shoot the aide's estranged husband to death, but the plan quickly fell apart and resulted in a scandalous trial and convictions for all involved. The shocking events, which rocked the community, were later turned into a 1996 mini-series titled *Seduced by Madness*.

What, if anything, is plaguing Paradise Road is unknown, but that might be part of the draw to the isolated country road. Online paranormal discussion boards are filled with photos and video from thrill-seekers each hoping to uncover the mysteries of this road. Meanwhile, area residents work closely with the Jefferson police to deter the curious by reporting trespassers and those whose adventure-seeking disturbs the peace of this remote road.

THE SUNSET PLAYHOUSE THEATRE:
800 ELM GROVE ROAD, ELM GROVE

A group of suburban actors banded together in 1954 to create the Sunset Playhouse, a nonprofit community theater group. By 1960, the group was able to open the doors of its Elm Grove Road location. The tightknit group of actors transformed the simple building erected on swampy land into a destination for western Milwaukee–area actors and theater lovers.

Among the favorite players of this era was Lester Schultz, known to his friends as "Pinky." Schultz, a former Marine and family man, was known in life to be a playful, lighthearted prankster. A frequent performer at the theater, he was an integral and much beloved part of the Sunset Playhouse. Tragically, Pinky had a sudden heart attack during a performance of *The Odd Couple* in 1968. Pinky, cast as the mild-mannered poker buddy Vinnie, lost his life in front of the audience, on stage right.

To honor the memory of the beloved actor, the group planted a tree on the grounds. The pink petals that bloom from the branches each spring are a continued reminder of the joy he brought to others. Not content to be just a pleasant memory in the theater, it seems as if Pinky remains in the building. Considered a fun-loving spirit, Pinky continues to be a welcome member of the Sunset group. The movement of props and misplacement of costumes are often attributed to him, and some Playhouse members have claimed to

The entryway of the popular suburban theater. *Author's collection.*

see his apparition. Regarded as a benevolent specter, observers are delighted when they catch a glimpse of Pinky in the theater. Reports claim that he is dressed in a sports jacket and still wears the warm, friendly smile so familiar to his fellow actors.

The Sunset Playhouse cheerfully acknowledges Pinky's presences, including mentions of him in theater programs and connecting his mischievous spirit with production mishaps. Many believe that Schultz is not the only spirit joyfully remaining at the theater. It is also believed that Roger Casey, a longtime volunteer at the theater, is still present. In 2008, then board member Jim Stankovsky participated in a paranormal investigation of the theater. One of the most exciting revelations of the investigation was the face of the deceased Roger Casey, caught on film, in the window of the light and sound booth in the theater. While the presence of the men was never questioned by Sunset Playhouse regulars, the results of the investigation seemed to present enough evidence of their presence that the spirits have gained legions of new believers.

DEACON WEST OCTAGON HOME: 370 HIGH STREET, PEWAUKEE

The strange octagonal home built by Pewaukee blacksmith Josiah West was completed in 1856. Built by West to replace his log cabin, he painstakingly created the eighteen-inch-thick walls of the eleven-room home himself. Those thick walls are the only thing that prevented a fire in 1873 from destroying the home. Perched on the town's only hill, the unusual home has invariably attracted attention in this small town.

There have always been gossip and rumors about the home. One claim about the home that has persisted through the years is that it is haunted. In the modern era, a series of homeowners had experiences that seem to support this claim. It may be that the home has always been the site of unexplained occurrences, but it wasn't until the 1900s that owners of the home went public with these mysterious happenings. Two separate families reported ghostly evening walks through the home. When the Hyle family owned the home, Mrs. Hyle claimed to hear disembodied footsteps on the second floor of the home that began each night precisely at 10:45 p.m.

When the Zupet family owned the home in the 1930s, Mrs. Zupet reported that the nocturnal walker began at 10:45 p.m. each night and ended at 1:20 a.m. She reported that the footsteps would continue through each room on

A view of the Deacon West Octagon Home. *Author's collection.*

the second floor, pausing only at windows and doorways. So unnerved was she by the disembodied footfalls that she had the linoleum floor covered in thick carpet in the hopes of muting the disturbing sounds. The carpeting did not help, and the family, unable to cope with the nightly activity in the home, moved within three years of purchasing it. When interviewed about the experience years later, Mrs. Zupet's daughter-in-law claimed to be skeptical about her mother-in-law's claims but did admit that when she spent the night in the home, she shared her bed with her children, as the home was frightening in the dark.

The Kirley family spoke about the haunting in the 1980s. The matriarch of the home reported that when her children were younger, they would often report ghostly sightings, mysterious banging and other frightening happenings. A group of the Kirley children reporting seeing a vaporous apparition fly through the home in the 1970s. The family remember a time when they left the windows of the home open to air a freshly painted room. While the family was out, a rainstorm passed over the home. The Kirleys dreaded seeing the damage they imagined the rain caused to the room. When they arrived home, they were stunned; all the windows in the home were tightly closed. With every member of the family out of the house, they had no idea how the windows became closed in their absence. Discussing this unusual occurrence with a neighbor, the neighbor reported seeing a man inside the home closing each window. No other man had access to this home. Might it have been Deacon West, helping the family currently caring for his house?

No one knows the origin of these strange occurrences. The persistent (yet unsubstantiated) story is that Deacon Josiah West killed his wife in the home, and her restless spirit is the source of the home's paranormal activity. Naysayers are quick to offer explanations for the strange occurrences, claiming that the speaking tubes embedded in the walls, used as an early form of an intercom system, are the source for the strange noises, along with the normal creaks of an aging home. One wonders if that explanation fully addresses loud banging in the home or footsteps that begin and end with clockwork precision. Additionally, these tubes do not begin to address the ghostly sightings in the home. Even those who have gone on record saying the home is not haunted claim that it is still a scary place to be at night. Perhaps they sense something their eyes will not let them see?

The Dousman Stagecoach Inn Museum: 1075 Pilgrim Parkway, Brookfield

Built by Talbot Dousman in 1842, the Dousman Stagecoach Inn once proudly sat at the corners of Bluemound and Watertown Plank Roads on a wagon road that had been adapted from a Native American trail. A rural location at the time, the area started to develop when the construction of the plank road began in 1848. By 1853, the fifty-eight-mile plank road had been completed, and the need for lodging to serve weary travelers had increased significantly. The Dousman Inn was converted to the Stagecoach Inn in 1857 by new owner Daniel Brown, and he enjoyed years of success until 1875, when the implementation of the railroad line dramatically decreased the need for stagecoaches, along with the businesses that served them. The stately double-porched building quietly became a farmhouse and then was donated to the City of Brookfield in 1980. It was moved to its new location on Pilgrim Parkway in 1981, where it now operates as a museum. It is believed that more was relocated that day than just the wood and nails used to construct the inn. It is thought the spirits that long occupied the building remain attached to it, despite its change of location.

Once a bustling inn, the building now serves as a museum. *Author's collection.*

Rumors of a haunting have surrounded this building for years and only intensified when it became a museum and people had increased access to the inn as well as the spirits that seem to dwell there. Those who visit the former Stagecoach Inn have reported doors slamming from an invisible hand, cold spots around the barn and inside the inn and orbs all over the property. Several have witnessed a dark figure pacing in the upper hallway. A French paranormal investigating team visited the inn and captured what it believes to be a ghostly image surrounded by a ball of light while photographing the inside the building.

Many visitors have claimed to have been shoved by an unseen spirit. Some have even claimed to have been pushed off the porch entirely by an unwelcoming entity. When interviewed about the supernatural occurrences in the home, Elmbrook Historical Society board member Lynda Thayer stated that she had no knowledge of the brutish spirit apt to shove guests but did relay a number of unexplained occurrences that could be attributed to a friendlier being. She reported having a closed door open for her as she stood before the door with her arms filled with boxes. A volunteer, standing on a chair to decorate for an event in the building, lost her balance, yet before she toppled from the chair, she felt herself steadied by benevolent, unseen hands.

A small group touring the master bedroom on the second floor was startled to see the rocking chair moving by itself in the room. While Thayer was quick to point out that it is possible the vibrations made from people walking on the well-worn wooden floors caused the chair to move, it is just as easy to assume that the helpful spirit collaborating with those in the museum may have just been observed taking a break in the rocking chair.

Several people have died in the building, but none tragically, so it is unknown who the spirit or spirits are that remain in the Dousman Stagecoach Inn. The grounds, which now consist of several outbuildings and an old schoolhouse in addition to the inn, are frequently used for Civil War reenactment activities. It may be this strong connection to the past that keeps the inn occupied by otherworldly visitors. The spirits seem quite comfortable on the grounds and show no signs of leaving any time soon.

HOTEL GRAFTON: 1312 WISCONSIN AVENUE, GRAFTON

This building in Grafton's quaint downtown area has been many things: a hotel, a restaurant, an apartment building and, it seems, a longtime home for spirits. Built in 1892, the Queen Anne–style hotel constructed of Cream City brick was designed to be an oasis for those traveling between Milwaukee and Sheboygan. A onetime tour stop for traveling musicians, the Hotel Grafton has hosted a wide variety of bands, some of which seem to have enjoyed playing there so much that they have never left.

The lettering and brickwork of the former hotel remind visitors of how the building looked before it was modernized. *Author's collection.*

22

There have been numerous reports of music playing despite the building being empty. Some hear orchestral music from a ballroom long closed, and others hear mourning blues riffs delivered from a stage in the distant past pouring out onto the sidewalk outside the building. All those who hear the music agree on one thing: it appears that an unseen party continues at the Hotel Grafton.

The reports of paranormal activity increased in the years the hotel was used as a restaurant. Guest rooms were converted into banquet rooms, and the once bustling uppers floors were no longer in use. These changes may have spurred the spirits to communicate with the living. Restaurant employees reported cabinets opening and closing on their own and the sound of footsteps crossing abandoned rooms and in empty stairwells. Some employees have witnessed a white, misty figure in the basement of the building. It is unknown whether this entity is responsible for the interactions with the staff or just one of the many spirits that have chosen not to check out of the Hotel Grafton.

The Rainbow Springs Curse: County Road LO, Mukwonago

Few people want anything as much as developer Francis Schroedel wanted to create the Rainbow Springs Resort. In 1959, Schroedel purchased nine hundred acres of land in Mukwonago with the dream of creating an elegant convention center filled with every amusement a sporting man could desire. Initially, he created a private club featuring a golf course and game hunting and later adding swimming and skiing to the list of activities club members could enjoy. All the while, he was making plan to open the resort of his dreams. By 1966, the developer had secured an $8 million loan, and the construction of the resort was soon underway. The multimillionaire builder had a thirty-eight years of experience in the Milwaukee area and an excellent reputation. It seemed that success was imminent.

By 1967, the financial climate had changed, and investors began backing out of the deal. With $12 million of his own money already invested in the property, Schroedel looked to a local bank for help when threats of foreclosure loomed from unpaid claim holders. Despite his precarious position, the developer resisted efforts of interested investors wanting to enter into a partnership in the resort. They had the money he needed, but the idea of relinquishing any form of control, or a percentage of the

A decaying building on the grounds of the ill-fated Rainbow Springs Resort, which was spared from the 2002 fire. *Author's collection*.

future profits he never stopped dreaming of, was impossible. Schroedel was determined to go it alone.

In November 1968, construction was completed. The massive building contained 7 grand ballrooms, 756 rooms and all the trappings of a modern convention center. Yet the complex, surrounded by a three-mile walking trail, stood vacant. Schroedel was out of money and desperately needed $2 million to complete the project. The beautifully built rooms were carpetless, and the hotel only had one telephone, forcing the developer to conduct all of his business from a dark corner in the on-site bar. The bank would offer no more money to the project, and Schroedel was out of personal funds. Despite the desperate situation, Francis Schroedel refused to stray from his original plans to develop the most elegant resort ever seen in Wisconsin.

While things crumbled around him, he continued to outfit himself in the finest European clothing, holding on to the dream of the grand opening of the resort where Sinatra would entertain. Supporters begged him to cut corners, to rescale his vision to match the situation, but he ignored all the well-meaning advice. Out of necessity, the developer and his wife made the vacant resort their home. Each day, the situation grew more financially precarious until, finally in 1973, the bank foreclosed on the never completed hotel.

Schroedel fought vehemently against the foreclosure, to no avail. The angry, broken man had to be forced from the property when it fell into the hands of the bank. More than one person heard the angry man state, "If I can't open it, no one will." Many believe those words were a promise as well as a curse. Schroedel died in 1976, remaining involved in a legal and financial battle over the still vacant and incomplete Rainbow Springs Resort.

Over the years, several businesses have tried to take over the property, to no avail. The property has a legacy of broken deals, tax liens and bankrupted investors, and it has still not welcomed its first guest. On April 16, 2002, amid rumors another takeover was in the works, a late-night fire of mysterious origin started on the property. More than two hundred firefighters from eighteen different departments worked into the next afternoon to put out the fire. Buildings were knocked down to prevent the fire from spreading. The suspicious fire was investigated, but the cause of the devastating blaze remained inconclusive.

Rainbow Springs Resort never opened, and the fire destroyed any hope that the complex would ever be completed. Over the years, every investor who tried to complete the Rainbow Springs project failed and was left worse off for the effort. Was it an ill-conceived project destined to fail from the start, or is Francis Schroedel, from beyond the grave, making good on his promise that no one but him will ever open the Rainbow Springs Resort? Today, the buildings that remain on the property are rotting, and it appears that the fields and forests on which they were built are reclaiming the structures. The once paved roads are gradually reverting to gravel, and birds and other wild animals are the only ones enjoying the once nearly complete luxury resort.

Winslow Elementary School: 1325 Park Avenue, Racine

The school located on Park Avenue in Racine was known as the Third Ward School when it was constructed in 1855. Built of Cream City brick, the High Victorian/Italianate construction underwent major renovations in 1897. Renamed for Horatio Gates Winslow, a former Racine school superintendent, the Southside Historic District school was added to the National Register of Historic Places in 1977.

Today, the building, still in use, looks to be a stately reminder of the past, but it had an inauspicious beginning. Despite being a much-anticipated addition to rapidly growing Racine, the location selected for the school

An interior view of a Racine schoolroom. *Library of Congress.*

was problematic. The spot chosen for the school was an existing cemetery. Officials had the bodies exhumed and relocated to the then new Mound Cemetery, so named because it was the site of an Indian burial mound. The exhumation was executed with questionable thoroughness; to this day, it is suspected that bodies are still underground on the school property.

Local lore claims that in the early days of the school, human bones would occasionally find their way to the surface of the playground, particularly in the area around the school's well. Students pumping water from this outdoor well would call the water "skeleton juice." The stories, and perhaps the bones of early residents, remained, and students continued to call water drawn from the school well by its spooky nickname even after indoor water fountains were added and city water was piped to the school.

The creepy tales of the school were not confined to discovery of mysterious bones. Over the years, there have been countless reports of footsteps heard from empty halls and voices calling from empty classrooms. Many have claimed to see dark apparitions passing by the windows of the vacant school as they viewed the school from outside the building. Tantalizingly unknown are the reasons a veteran custodian at the school refused to enter the boiler room. What might he have experienced in that room that made him determined to never enter again? Since it was built, the school has been an integral part of the Southside neighborhood, and at the heart of some of its best folklore, and it will likely continue to play those roles well into the future.

THE TWO MARYS: MARY BUTH HOMESTEAD, GERMANTOWN

In 1966, Tom Walton, the owner at the time of the Mary Buth homestead in Germantown, gave an interview to a news reporter about some frightening occurrences that happened on the property. Instantly, Mary Buth became the most popular, discussed, feared and sought-after ghost that ever roamed the Washington County countryside. Depending on whom you believe, Mary Buth is long dead and either resting comfortably in the private Buth cemetery, or her bones remain in the yard of the Buth homestead. Regardless of where her remains lie, many believe that her spirit lingers on the grounds, forever filled with longing and desperately seeking something.

Founded in 1838 by John and Mary Buth, the Mary Buth homestead sits close to the intersection of Mary Buth Road and Lovers Lane. The home still contains the original log structure that was part of an Indian trading post. The farming family were among the first white settlers to the area and, from all accounts, led an uneventful life of hard work and religious virtue. The couple had six children, with three surviving to adulthood. For Mary, life was made significantly more difficult when her husband died, leaving her a widow to manage the farm and provide for her family. Mary lived out the

The road marker of this legendary rural lane. *Author's collection.*

remainder of her life at the rural outpost, leaving the mortal coil in 1899, surrounded by her surviving children: her sons Carl and Herman, as well as daughter and namesake Mary.

The Buth children were an odd lot. None of the surviving children ever married, and the three of them remained together until they each died one by one. Not that their existence on the farm was particularly peaceful. It is said that brothers Carl (1839–1923) and Herman (1849–1917), despite living in the same house, did not speak to each other. While both men were alive, they used little sister Mary (1850–1926) as an intermediary. Lonely Mary, known for her piety and volunteerism, was kept company by what has been described as "swarms" of cats. Leaving the homestead after the death of Carl, she is the only Buth not to die on the farm. In death, the family is again united in a private cemetery, which is currently under the care of the Germantown Historical Society.

So, how did these pioneering women become the source of so many campfire tales and late-night dares? On New Year's Eve 1965, the Waltons hosted a party. Despite all the trappings of a great event, the hosts still had a sense of uncomfortable foreboding as their guests began to arrive. The Waltons noted small, strange things as they circulated the rooms containing revelers. Candles seemed to be burning much more quickly that night. The television and other electrical appliances seemed to be acting up, shutting themselves off suddenly without cause. The couple also noted unexpected cold spots in the visitor-filled rooms. During this unsettling night, the focus of the party very suddenly turned when Tom Walton spotted a gnarled old woman peering into the window of his home. The stranger, clad in a rough-hewn black dress, startled Walton into stupefaction. By the time he was able to react, the woman had disappeared. Investigating the scene the next morning, Walton noticed an absence of footprints outside the window but discovered that the plant in the sill of that window was completely dead on the exterior side; the side of the plant that faced the party remained green and healthy. Walton was puzzled and curious.

The events of that night seemed to initiate a series of strange events in the home. Soon, a plumber working alone in the home claimed to hear footfalls on the floor above him. Confused by the sounds, he checked the second floor, only to confirm that he was the only one in the house. Later, an overnight guest claimed to see a woman clad in white disappear into the misty yard early one morning. Walton was perplexed by the report, as the remote homestead has few neighbors—and none close enough to get a glimpse of from inside the home. Eventually, the Walton family hired a psychic to investigate the home. The psychic stated there were two spirits in the dwelling: both Mary Buths. This fit with Walton's longtime belief that the women roamed the homestead in the day and came into the house each night. When the psychic probed further, she felt that a darkness had entered the younger Mary and her mother was protecting the home from her daughter.

The reason the cat-loving spinster might be an evil force on the farm is elusive and ultimately remains unknown. All lasting accounts of the farm's lone daughter present a woman who was kind, patient and hardworking. Unsubstantiated town legends claim that young Mary's heart may have been broken by a traveling salesman who left her at the altar. The reports of Mary sightings planted by Walton in his 1966 interview reaped much fruit. Since then, the legend of Mary has grown. Rather than merely lovelorn, the Mary Buth of today's stories is angry and dangerous. Seeking her is a perilous challenge that the curious take on with zeal. Some people claim to see an apparition of Mary riding a carriage down Mary Buth Lane. Others claim that a younger Mary, in white, and her mother, in black, can both be seen slinking around the farm grounds. Those most determined to connect with Mary seek the small graveyard on the property, a spot impossible to access without trespassing on private land.

As the rumors about how the spirits manifest themselves at the farm grow more fantastic, there has been a dramatic increase in late-night thrill-seekers coming to the property in hopes of experiencing the supernatural phenomena for themselves. For the living who make the homestead their home, this unwelcome attention has caused them to increase their security measures and the Germantown police to increase their patrols in the area, where they have often issued tickets for trespassing, disturbing the peace and underage drinking.

Does young Mary Buth rest uneasily because of a lost love? Is her mother still caring for the property and those in it from beyond the grave? Many think so, and the reported evidence suggests that there could be something left of these women in this historic home. Harder to believe are the claims that either of these spirits will seek out the living or harm them. It is difficult to think that the nature of the Buth women would be so changed by death that their actions would so dramatically diverge from how they behaved when living. Whatever the final analysis on the spirits that linger on the land, it is paramount to remember that the Mary Buth homestead and the Buth cemetery are both private property and that trespassing is expressly forbidden.

SUPERSTAR SPECTERS

MILWAUKEE'S MOST FAMOUS GHOSTS AND HAUNTS

The Brew City loves to embrace tradition and celebrate time-tested classics. These well-known spirits and spooky locations have tingled the spines of generations of Milwaukeans, and no collection of Milwaukee ghost stories would be complete without them.

THE SPECTER OF *SOPRA MARE*: VILLA TERRACE, 2220 NORTH TERRACE AVENUE, MILWAUKEE

It is not entirely unexpected to hear the sounds of children's laughter or the scampering of little feet through the halls of Villa Terrace—after all, it has been a museum since 1966. Additionally, it wasn't at all uncommon to hear children at play when Lloyd R. Smith, president of A.O. Smith Corporation, built this home for his family in 1923.

What *is* unexpected is the longtime source of these playful sounds. She is a lovely child, with flowing locks of long blond hair, and is clad in a powder blue dress. Legend has it that this little girl has been playing in the Mediterranean manor since it was built.

When the six Smith children were young, they shared more than the exquisite Italian Renaissance home perched majestically above Lake Michigan that the family called *Sopra Mare*; they also shared an imaginary playmate. At least, the famed industrialist and his wife, Agnes, assumed

The celebrated Neptune Gate at the eastern entrance to the garden. *Author's collection.*

she was imaginary. After all, they could not see her. With their dear friend in the blue dress, the children raced down hallways together and played hide-and-seek in the mansion's many rooms. Occasionally, the adults in the home thought they might have caught a glimpse of the children's fair-haired companion out of the corner of their eyes, but they dismissed it, just as they did the sounds of a child's footfalls in the corridors after all of the Smith children were soundly sleeping.

Time passed, and the six children became five when young Robert died at age nine. As the children grew, they spent less and less time with their spritely friend. One by one, the children became adults and left the home. The children's mother, Agnes, was the sole occupant of the home after patriarch Lloyd died of a heart attack in 1944. In the big home, it was just Agnes—and the young girl in blue who ran through the halls looking for a willing playmate.

It is not known if Agnes saw the girl in the years after her own children left home, but the girl is still very much a part of Villa Terrace to this day. Who the impish girl in blue is, and why she has chosen the mansion as her playground, remains a mystery. Visitors and staff have claimed to see her in

The internal courtyard when the museum was still a private residence. *Library of Congress.*

the museum, reporting sightings all over the former home. Forever young and lively, she still races the halls in her blue frock, seeking companions for the games she's been playing in the home since the 1920s. Those who have had encounters with her say she disappears as suddenly as she appears, leaving nothing but a mass of icy air in her wake.

THE MODJESKA THEATER:
1134 WEST HISTORIC MITCHELL STREET, MILWAUKEE

The Modjeska Theater on Milwaukee's Southside was once a movie palace that also attracted popular vaudeville acts. Built in 1924 and named in honor of famed Polish stage actress Madame Helena Modjeska (1840–1909), the theater was known to screen Polish-language films for its largely Polish neighbors. While a historically important landmark, today the Modjeska may be best known as one of Milwaukee's most mysteriously haunted theaters. There seems little doubt that the theater is haunted; the mystery is whose spirit still lingers in the theater and why.

The theater's most frequently seen apparition has been named Balcony Man by generations of theatergoers. He is often spotted sitting in the balcony, attired in a top hat, looking down at the stage. Those who have seen him report that the figure appears as a white haze, sometimes described as a "foggy" or "smoky" presence hovering in the seats of the gallery. Who this spectral audience member is remains unknown. Some believe his presence is connected to a fire that destroyed the original Modjeska Theater. The first Modjeska, built in 1910, was a considerably smaller theater than the one patrons enjoy today. Badly damaged in a fire, the old theater was destroyed and replaced. Persistent neighborhood gossip suggested that the fire's origin may not have been accidental. The hazy balcony dweller began to be seen shortly after the new theater was opened. Rumors of a suspicious fire, coupled with the appearance of the mysterious, smoky specter, caused patrons to believe that the ghostly audience member was somehow linked to the fire.

While the Balcony Man is the best-known spirit lingering in the Modjeska, in a 2017 interview, former theater owner Judy Smith revealed that the theater was home to three restless souls. According to her, the active entities make themselves known using icy blasts of air. It is not uncommon for those backstage, particularly in the long office hallways, to walk through cold spots or feel a cold touch on the neck or arm, alerting them to the presence of these spirits.

The benign spirits are happy to live peacefully with those occupying the building. The souls have been with the theater for such a long time that they are now as much a part of this landmark as the showy balcony stair rails or the detailed plasters in the lobby. The long seen and felt dwellers are likely pleased that renovations are underway to ensure that this theater is once again an essential part of the Southside. As the Modjeska Theater finds new life in its restoration, it appears certain that new generations of theatergoers will experience their own ghostly sightings.

MUIRDALE SANATORIUM:
TECHNOLOGY INNOVATION CENTER, 10437 INNOVATION DRIVE

Tuberculosis was the scourge of the early twentieth century. With the development of antibiotics years off, the only treatment was sunlight, fresh air and nutritious foods. This course of treatment left 50 percent of those subjected to it dead within five years of the initial diagnosis. At the turn of the century, 450 Americans died per day of the disease, commonly known as consumption.

The urban poor were most afflicted with this highly contagious, airborne disease marked by a chronic cough, fever, rapid weight loss and night sweats. Patients were plagued with mucous-filled lungs—the thick, white phlegm expectorated by the patients' bone-rattling coughs earned the disease the terrifying moniker the "White Plague." The persistent coughing damaged the patient's airways, making it very common for patients to cough up blood, giving a clear indication that the infected were suffering from more than a severe chest cold.

The highly contagious nature of the disease lead to the development of sanatoriums. These treatment centers, most often in rural, isolated areas, served not only to protect the general population from the infection but also to provide the ample fresh air it was believed the afflicted needed to be cured of the dreaded disease. It was those goals that led to the opening of Muirdale Sanatorium on what was then known as the Country Institution Grounds in Wauwatosa. Named for famed Wisconsin naturalist John Muir, the sanatorium opened in 1915. At its peak, it was able to house 770 patients, and the grounds saw more than 10,000 tuberculosis patients between 1915 and 1936.

As medical technology progressed, the need for grounds to isolate tuberculosis became unnecessary. In 1970, the facility was renamed Rehab West and was used as a place to house the elderly with mental illnesses. Finally closed in 1978, it is unknown how many died in the sixty-three years the facility housed those in need. This final home for countless Milwaukeeans was designated a landmark in 1980.

Now known as the Technology Innovation Center, the building is home to more than forty area businesses. While some remodeling has been done, the echoes of its past present themselves all over the building. On the outside, the building retains its stately, institutional look, which is a particularly stark contrast to its modern neighbors in Research Park. Inside, the building boasts some impressive technical capabilities, as well as many structural nods from its days as a treatment facility.

An external view of the former tuberculosis ward. *Author's collection.*

Perhaps it is those familiar interiors that keep spirits connected to this building. The sounds of disembodied coughing can be heard on all floors of the building. Those who spend time on the third floor have reported hearing cries for help, and fifth-floor dwellers are plagued by doors slammed by an unseen hand. Not only can the sounds of the past be detected in the building, but so can its previous occupants. Ghostly apparitions have been seen on all floors of the building. Most reports are glimpses of former patients roaming through the halls or unexpectedly appearing in former treatment rooms, now used as offices.

The fifth floor of the building seems to be particularly active. One person employed in the building claims to have been working late one night when he entered what he believe to be an empty conference room, only to discover a ghostly figure in a nurse's uniform. Nighttime visitors to the grounds claim to see what they believe are the faces of former patients looking out fifth-floor windows. Strange occurrences in the building are not confined to the nighttime hours though. Daytime visitors often report seeing figures move from the corner of the eye, only to turn and find nothing there. In the hallways, people sense an unseen presence and have the feeling they are never truly alone in the building.

THE PABST MANSION:
2000 WEST WISCONSIN AVENUE, MILWAUKEE

Beer baron Captain Frederick Pabst (1863–1904) is among Milwaukee's most celebrated citizens. The successful mariner purchased an interest in his father-in-law's brewery in 1864. From there, he began his domination of the Brew City and beyond. As his empire expanded, the need for a spectacular home befitting one of the city's most prominent citizens presented itself. Construction of the stunning Pabst Mansion began in 1890 on Grand Avenue. The spectacular 20,019-square-foot, five-level home boasted sixty-six rooms when it was completed in 1892.

The Pabst family's tenure of the palatial home was short. The captain died in 1904, and his widow, Maria, followed in 1906. Once located in the toniest part of town, the area was now less desirable to the smart set, whose mansions now lined the lakefront. After remaining vacant for two years, the home finally found a new owner; in 1908, the Catholic Archdiocese of Milwaukee purchased the home as the residence for the archbishop. The

The former home of beer baron Captain Frederick Pabst and his wife, Maria. *Author's collection.*

mansion remained with the church until 1975, when it was deemed too costly to maintain. For some time, it appeared that the Pabst Mansion would suffer the same fate as did most of its former neighbors: demolition. The historic home narrowly avoided being razed to make way for a parking lot when it was saved in 1978 and turned into a museum.

Thousands of visitors each year visit the popular tourist attraction. Many of the guests arrive hoping to see the home's exquisite craftsmanship and others to step into back into the opulent splendor of the Victorian era. Then there are those who come to make a connection with the home's most famous former occupant: Captain Frederick Pabst.

Those who spend the most time in the home, staff and volunteers, have compiled quite a collection of supernatural happenings since the home has been a museum. Over the years, people have witnessed the heavy, ornately carved, solid wood doors opening and closing on their own. Objects are known to fall from tables onto the floor without any human intervention. Those moving through the house have reported feeling unexplained cold breezes and strange cold spots in the home. One late March evening, the volunteers were busily preparing for an event in the museum. As a worker was making the final arrangements in the room, it was noticed that the unlit candles had fallen out of the candelabra. Securing the candles back into the holder, the volunteer was called out of the room. When she returned, the candles were again out of the holders and on the ground. The vintage fixture had been used for years without incident, so this problem was puzzling. Discussing this strange happening with another worker, it was noticed that the day was Captain Pabst's birthday, March 28. Was this mischievous candle play Pabst's way of "blowing out" his birthday candles from beyond the grave?

The stories most often retold by those who work in the mansion are the stories of frustrated tradesmen at the property to do repair or restoration work on the home. For years, a long line of those hired to work on house have been bothered by a man who is overly interested in the work being done. The man, described as older, with a full mustache and prominent goatee, will hover over the workers, often interfering with their work. When the tradesperson mentions the bothersome man to mansion workers, it soon becomes clear that the meddlesome observer is none other than the original owner of the home, Frederick Pabst, still carefully overseeing the details of his magnificent home.

St. Joan of Arc Chapel: Marquette University Campus (Enter Courtyard at 14ᵗʰ Street, by Library)

Milwaukee's oldest mystery began in Chasse, France, sometime in the fifteenth century. Likely sometime around 1420, a church was built in honor of St. Martin de Seyssuel. The Gothic-style church in southeastern France was used as a local place of worship for hundreds of years, but by the late 1700s, the time of the French Revolution, it had fallen into disrepair and then was largely abandoned. The historic and architectural gem was rediscovered in the twentieth century, and restoration efforts began in 1920.

Once the restoration on church was completed, it was purchased by American socialite and Francophile Gertrude Hill Gavin. She had the church fully dismantled and shipped, stone by stone, to her Long Island property, where she had the church reassembled next to a French chateau that had also been relocated to the property. Gavin, a devotee of Ste. Jeanne d'Arc, had the church renamed in honor of the heroic patron of France.

It is easy to see why Gavin was a follower of the fascinating Maid of Orleans. St. Joan (1412–1431) was like any pious farm girl in rural France

The tiny chapel fits snugly in the courtyard of the urban campus. *Author's collection.*

until she started receiving divine messages when she turned thirteen years old. Joan's first message told her to follow God and he would help her. Time passed, and the frequency of the messages grew. In her eighteenth year, she received daily messages from God, the Virgin Mary, St. Michael, St. Catherine and St. Margaret. Many of the messages urged her to lead the French army and help Charles VII to seize the crown. She met with Charles VII to tell him of what she believed was God's plan and her role in it. She convinced him that her messages were divine by revealing something to him that no one other than God would know. The details of the conversation have never been divulged, but Charles was convinced and sent the teenaged Joan off to battle, leading French troops on her white horse, clad in white armor.

Joan aided France in its victory over the English in the Hundred Years' War, but for unknown reasons, the newly crowned Charles did not help Joan when she fell into enemy hands. She was jailed, branded a heretic and ultimately burned at the stake on May 30, 1431. Her enemies hoped that the execution of the nineteen-year-old girl would discredit her stories, but her martyrdom only made her more popular. The patron of France was officially made a Catholic saint in 1920, the same year the small church was rediscovered.

Whether Gavin was committed to St. Joan because of her critical role in French history or her spirituality is not well known. Regardless of the reasons, St. Joan was significant to Gavin, which was evident when she renamed her newly obtained church and later when she had a relic from her favorite saint installed in the fifteenth-century church. Found in France, Gavin purchased a stone it is believed that Joan kneeled on in prayer before going into battle. It is reported that Joan kissed the stone when she completed her prayer. Many believe that the stone is an earthly connection to the divine and has properties that reveal its otherworldliness. The stone touched by the saint, now part of the wall behind the altar, is said to be noticeably colder than all of the stones around it. To add further intrigue to the church, there are those who believe that St. Joan may have at one time prayed in the church, despite there being little historical evidence to support the claim.

Upon Gavin's death, the church became the property of noted local business executive and philanthropist Marc Rojtman, who donated it to Marquette University. Once again, the six-hundred-year-old church was dismantled and then reassembled in Milwaukee. The stone relic acquired by Gavin was reinstalled in the historic building. In 1966, the church was rebuilt and reopened to worshipers.

Today, the St. Joan of Arc Chapel is a frequently visited location on the Marquette campus. Some come to worship and others to view the historic building, but many come to get closer to St. Joan and to experience the mysteries of her stone. Longtime docent Julie Baumann added credence to the story of the cold stone, stating that each time the temperature of the St.

Joan's stone was measured it was between three and five degrees cooler than the surrounding stones. She further stated that many have examined the stone and surrounding areas, but none has been able to provide an explanation for the difference in temperature between the relic and the other stones. Whether Joan prayed in the church or kissed the stone the faithful flock to see will never be satisfactorily proven, but the attraction to the martyred girl and mystique of this medieval church will continue far into the future.

RIVERSIDE THEATER:
116 WEST WISCONSIN AVENUE, MILWAUKEE

When the Riverside Theater opened its doors in 1928, it was Milwaukee's favorite place to see vaudeville stars. Audiences filled the 2,460 seats to see the legendary Abbott and Costello and roar to the antics of the Three Stooges. When vaudeville died in the mid-1930s, it largely became a film house but still presented live shows featuring big stars of each era, including Judy Garland, Chuck Berry, Johnny Cash, Ray Charles and Bruce Springsteen. For most, the key attraction to the theater is the list of famous performers who have taken the stage, but for some, the paranormal occurrences in the concert hall make this a must-visit location for ghost seekers.

Paranormal enthusiasts Susan Scot Fry and Jason Gierl teamed up in 2011 to explore the unearthly happenings in this landmark. Together, the pair immersed themselves in documenting the happenings in the theater once the show was over and the audience had gone home. They gathered stories of unexplained events and conducted research in the theater, sharing what they learned with fans eager to learn more about the rumored haunting.

It is after hours that former Riverside employee Gierl had his first direct contact with a spirit in the theater. As the last one in the building, he was locking up for the evening when he heard a voice directly in his ear unmistakably say, "Hey." He knew it wasn't his imagination, as he could tell that his dog standing beside him heard it too. The dog was frozen in place and so terrified at hearing the disembodied voice that he was too frightened to walk and needed to be carried from the theater.

Gierl also reported that employees have had experiences with a former technician who has a playful sense of humor. Legend has it that in the 1930s, a projectionist working in the light room died of a heart attack. It is believed that the spirit of the man remains in the room, teasing the current employees.

The downtown theater plays host to a variety of traveling acts, attracting Milwaukeeans of all walks to its halls. *Author's collection.*

More than one member of the staff has reported turning off the stage lights in the light room and climbing down the many flights of stairs to get to stage level, only to find the lights back on. The confused employee will then again climb the stairs to reach the light room, only to find the stage lights are now shut off. The spirit of the room appears to be a prankster, as one round of this light play is rarely enough for him. Eventually, the employee is able to get the stage lights to remain off, but only after rushing up and down the many stairs countless times.

Susan Scot Fry, a self-described "haunt-a-holic," discovered that the theater was rife with cold spots and the sounds and shadows of those no longer in this realm. During her investigation, she uncovered reports of a blue light hovering in the hallway of the basement, as well as the sound of a guttural, animal-like growl coming from the subterranean machine room. In a nearby part of the basement, close to the icemaker, employees reported the feeling of being touched or tapped by an unseen entity.

Patrons of the theater have not been exempt from paranormal experiences. Both employees and guests have caught the scent of cigar smoke from an unseen smoker and sudden bursts of a strong floral perfume that seems to have no origin. Some claim to have seen the apparition of a man walking in the aisles of the theater when it is empty, sometimes pausing to recline in the plush red seats.

Much has been uncovered about the supernatural life of the Riverside Theater, and much remains to be discovered. Its rich history and proximity to the Milwaukee River seems to make it an attractive location for restless spirits.

THE RAVE/EAGLES CLUB: 2401 WEST WISCONSIN AVENUE, MILWAUKEE

Ask a Milwaukeean to list the haunted places in town, and the Rave/Eagles Club will likely be at the top of the list. Rumors swirl around this venue, and it seems as if everyone either knows someone who has had a ghostly sighting in the building or has a favorite band that had a supernatural encounter there while playing a show. A favorite spot for ghost hunters of all stripes, the musical venue is more famous for its hauntings than it is as a historical site, despite being named to the National Register of Historic Places in 1986.

An external view of what was one time the most celebrated Fraternal Order of Eagles Aerie in the nation. *Author's collection.*

The building officially opened under the name the Eagles Club on September 13, 1927. It was built as the Milwaukee headquarters (known as "an Aerie") for the Fraternal Order of Eagles. This charitable organization focused on social justice and was very active in the first part of the twentieth century. Milwaukee's interest in the organization was strong and at one time had the largest chapter in the United States. The Milwaukee headquarters was the grandest of all the Aeries and became the national headquarters for the organization in 1955. The club members enjoyed amenities like a two-story gymnasium, a bowling alley, a radio station and, of course, the much talked-about basement-level swimming pool.

Let's take a look at two of the often-told rumors about this popular venue.

Buddy Holly Haunts the Rave

Buddy Holly did kick off his final tour, known as Winter Dance Party, in what was then known as George Devine's Million Dollar Ballroom on January 23, 1959. The musicians then played eight additional shows in Wisconsin, Minnesota and Iowa before their last show in Clear Lake, Iowa, on February 2, 1959. After several brutal days on the road during an exceptionally cold winter, show headliners Buddy Holly, Richie Valens and J.P. "the Big Bopper" Richardson boarded a chartered plane in Iowa to fly to their next show in Moorehead, Minnesota, eager to avoid the ice-slicked roads, subzero temperatures and miserable conditions on the often broken tour bus. The decision was fateful, as the plane crashed, and the event has been known ever after as "the day the music died."

So, does Buddy Holly still roam the halls of the Rave? Who knows, but it seems unlikely that he would return to the start of the most miserable tour he ever played.

There Is the Ghost of a Young Girl in the Pool Area

The pool, long ago drained and locked away, is at the heart of many stories that surround the building. Crafty trespassers have managed to get into the off-limits area and created scores of YouTube videos of their adventures. Those who have entered the area have reported feeling the presence of a young girl, seeing orbs and even feeling someone trying to hold their hand. The videos, filmed in the dark and often inside the emptied pool, have a spooky aura, and it often appears that the ghost seekers on camera are genuinely afraid.

The pool was the location of a drowning. Fifteen-year-old Francis Wren drowned in the pool on September 10, 1927, at about 3:30 p.m. while swimming with some high school friends. The boy slipped beneath the water unnoticed and was discovered unresponsive under 9.5 feet of water. He was dead before he could be taken from the pool and was soon laid to rest at Holy Cross Cemetery on September 13. Tragically, the boy's heartbroken mother soon joined him at Holy Cross, as she died several weeks afterward and was buried next to him.

Visitors to the Rave have also reported hearing the sounds of unseen children playing. Some have reported seeing the apparition of a young girl in the area near the coatroom. After-hours janitorial crews have spotted groups of ghostly children. In contrast to these happy entities, there have been reports of a single child crying in the empty venue. Most disturbingly, there have been a number of reports of items being thrown from the roof of the building. When this is reported to security and investigated, there is no one ever found on the roof.

Today, the Rave is both one of Milwaukee's favorite concert venues and a favorite location to experience spine-tingling thrills—or at least seek them out. It's possible your next concert there might include a paranormal experience. Stranger things have happened, particularly at the Rave.

COURTING IN THE CAVES: HISTORIC MILLER CAVES, 3897 WEST STATE STREET, MILWAUKEE

An eternal love story plays out each night at the one of the city's most iconic breweries. When Frederick Miller purchased the failing Plank Road Brewery, it contained underground caves to keep the beer cold in the era before refrigeration. As Miller's business expanded, so did the caves, eventually becoming large enough to store twelve thousand barrels of beer. By 1906, mechanical refrigeration had eliminated the need for the caves.

While no longer needed as an integral part of the brewery, the caves, despite being closed, still saw a great many visitors. Workers who sought relief from the heat in a world before air conditioning found a break-time walk in the caves a welcome respite. Strolls were taken, lunches were eaten and, if you believe the gossip of brewery workers, trysts were had.

According to an oft-told tale, passed through generations of Miller employees, during a long-ago summer a young brewery worker and his sweetheart met each Saturday night at the mouth of the cave, in the rear off the brewery. On those evenings, they would walk through the cool, dark caves, hand in hand in the lantern light.

The couple happily passed the summer. One warm evening, the young woman stood waiting for her swain at the opening of the cave, as she did every Saturday. She smoothed her hair and dress in anticipation of his arrival. When he did not appear promptly, she thought perhaps he had work that needed to be finished and would be along shortly. Her anticipation grew to irritation as the minutes dragged on. The irritation turned to fear. Had his feelings changed? Had something happened? Distant church bells let her know that she had been waiting for more than an hour. With a heavy heart, she set off for home alone.

Once home, she learned that the young man had fallen in the staircase of the caves, striking his head and rendering him unconscious. She immediately rushed to his side. Sadly, her bedside vigil did not help; he died several days later, never regaining consciousness. Months later, the young woman was also dead. While the doctor diagnosed her with a lung ailment, many of the young man's former coworkers were convinced that she died of a broken heart.

Shortly after the death of the girl, brewery workers claimed to see two luminous figures shimmering at the cave's entrance. Other employees reported hearing bits of conversation and laughter from what appeared to be empty caves. Security guards follow sounds of footsteps in the dark caves, only to have them mysteriously disappear. These lovers, walking hand and hand through the dimly lit Miller caves, appear to remain forever young and in love in the hideaway they enjoyed so long ago.

The Baron on the Third Floor: Milwaukee Public Museum, 800 West Wells Street, Milwaukee

Still stealthily roaming its halls is the dashing and flamboyant former Milwaukee Public Museum director Dr. Stephan Francis Borhegyi (1921–1969). This remarkable man, often cited as one of the inspirations for the fictional character of Indiana Jones, was a swashbuckling archaeologist with a specialty in Maya culture. Awarded the directorship of the MPM in 1959, he was instrumental in the creation of one of the museum's most beloved exhibits, "The Streets of Old Milwaukee." His larger-than-life personality was accented by his predilection for wearing capes and theatrically smoking pipes. Born in Hungary, the intriguing Borhegyi held the aristocratic title of baron, which he inherited from his grandfather. Always a charmer, he was well known for delighting the ladies with his courtly manners and thrilling tales of his globe-trotting adventures.

Borhegyi's life came to an abrupt end on September 26, 1969, when he was involved in a fatal car accident just blocks from the museum. Many believe that the spirit of the doctor continued on to his office that day and still remains in the Milwaukee Public Museum. The third floor, where such South American treasures as shrunken heads from the Ecuadorian Jivaro tribe and Peruvian mummies can be found, is the place where countless members of the museum staff have had encounters with the former director.

Through the years, many have reported catching glimpses of a man in a cape out of the corner of their eye as they walk through the exhibits on the third floors. Others have reported hearing the sounds of hearty laughter and smelling the familiar scent of pipe tobacco as they move through his beloved collections. After hours, third-floor motion sensors often go off, seemingly by themselves. The elevator frequently arrives on the third floor, and the doors open, despite the lack of human intervention.

Perhaps the most interesting phenomenon that has been reported on the third floor are the physical interactions museum staff have had with the former director. Those who have sensed him in their presence describe the feeling of an intense chill that suddenly moves right through their bodies. Giving validity to these claims is Dawn Scher Thomae, a member of the MPM staff since 1987 who spoke with Marquette University reporter Laura Bulgrin in 2009. The curator described her encounter with Borhegyi as a sensation that "didn't come from above, it came right through me," adding that "it's a feeling you don't readily forget."

OLMSTED'S JEWEL: LAKE PARK, 2975 NORTH LAKE PARK ROAD, MILWAUKEE

There are few hauntings as mysterious as the ones surrounding Lake Park. Ask any Milwaukeean to direct you to haunted locations around town, and the North Point Lighthouse and Lion Bridge, both located in Lake Park, are certain to come up in the conversation. The lighthouse, built in 1855 and moved to its current location in 1888, was designed into Frederick Law Olmsted's famous park in 1893. The 28-foot tower soared 107 feet above Lake Michigan, making it the highest lighthouse on the Great Lakes when it was built. In 1897, Lion Bridge was completed, and the landmarks have been intertwined in the stories of paranormal activity ever since.

Visitors to the area often report feeling an overall sense of dread as they approach the path on either side of Lion Bridge. This feeling of being distinctly unwelcome in the area increases as the walker gets closer to the lighthouse. Reports of icy cold spots felt on both the bridge and inside and outside of the lighthouse have been reported, a sensation that is distinctly more terrifying during hot, muggy Milwaukee summers. Most perplexing to visitors are the ghostly children that linger in the area.

Faint sounds of the disembodied laughter of children can be heard in the areas around the lighthouse and the bridge. Strangely, when those who've heard the laughter describe it, it does not sound like the joyful laughter of children at play, but rather a sinister laughter that seems to be warning those who approach the area to proceed with caution. Groups of ghostly, menacing-looking children have been spotted on both sides of the bridge.

The seventy-four-foot-tall Northpoint Lighthouse on the grounds of Lake Park. *Author's collection.*

Many who have observed these apparitions indicate that the children look to be acting as guards in the area. Far from welcoming park-goers to the area, these spirits discourage all but the brave from visiting the oft-photographed area alone.

These ghostly encounters puzzle visitors. There was never a tragedy involving the death of a group of children in Lake Park. A look at the history of the property does not show any murders in the area or death of a number of children in a lighthouse keeper's family. The lack of a noted event tying these spirits to the area makes this a mystery to ghost seekers—that is, unless you consider that Lake Park was built on prehistoric Indian mounds.

It is unknown how many mounds were destroyed by early settlers to the area and, later, by the completion of the park. Plowed over for the land or plundered by relic seekers, there was little effort made to preserve these spiritually significant lands. Just one prehistoric Indian mound remains in Lake Park today. Not much is known about the people who built this mound. It is thought that a Mid-Woodland Culture created the landmarks sometime between 300 BC and AD 400. The mounds were likely used either as burial sites or as ceremonial centers. At one time, there were perhaps twenty thousand sacred mounds in Wisconsin, with only an estimated four thousand remaining. The Lake Park prehistoric Indian mound is one of the two that can be found in Milwaukee County.

Many believe that the destruction of these sacred spots is the source of the spiritual unrest in the park. Perhaps the backhoes that created the park and the pickaxes that searched the mounds unearthed more than just bones and pottery shards. Are these ghostly children protecting an area sacred to them or attempting to frighten those they see as responsible for disturbing the mounds? Who these children are and why they linger in the park remains unknown, but it is likely that they will continue to be there as long as the Northpoint Lighthouse and the Lion Bridge remain in Lake Park.

MILWAUKEE'S MOST FAMOUSLY HAUNTED BUILDING AND ITS FAVORITE HOST: THE PFISTER HOTEL, 424 EAST WISCONSIN AVENUE, MILWAUKEE

Perhaps Milwaukee's most famous ghost is perennial host Charles F. Pfister. Born in 1859 in New York, Charles and his sister, Louisa, were adopted by tannery owner and capitalist Guido Pfister and his wife. The well-loved

An external view of the luxurious Pfister Hotel. *Author's collection.*

children were the wealthy and influential couple's sole heirs, and both became an integral part of the Pfister business holding and Milwaukee history. While today Charles Pfister is remember primarily as an hotelier, he was heavily invested in railroads, utilities and real estate and was a nationally known Republican stalwart.

Guido Pfister had a dream to build Milwaukee's most luxurious hotel, the Hotel Pfister, but died before his dream was realized. Dutiful son Charles made certain that Guido's vision became a reality. Opened in 1893, the hotel was the "first class, fire proof" structure the family wanted it to be. With a solid construction, electricity and in-room thermostats, an unheard-of luxury in the day, it was Milwaukee's finest hotel as well as one of the Midwest's best. The beautiful, marble-filled, gilded hotel became a magnet for politicians and celebrities traveling to Milwaukee.

Unlike most of Pfister's holding, the hotel was not an initial success. Undeterred, Charles Pfister threw elaborate banquets and balls to bring in prominent guests and expand the opulent hotel's reputation. Pfister, an exacting man of fastidious habits, was dogmatic about the service offered to guests. The owner was determined that guests would experience a level of hospitality that matched the unparalleled surroundings. Never one to shirk duties, Pfister was often found in the lobby of the hotel, personally greeting guests. He made the hotel his primary residence and moved into the hotel a large private collection of Victorian art. In 1927, he suffered stroke, after which he developed a complication that would cause his death on November 12. It was during that year that the never-married Pfister sold the hotel to longtime Hotel Pfister employee Ray Smith. The man who started his career at the hotel as a bellboy in 1896 assured the ailing Pfister that he would continue to run the hotel as it had been run. Pfister died at his sister Louisa Vogel's Lake Drive home, also the location of his funeral. After his death, he was celebrated not only as a shrewd and politically active business man but also as a generous philanthropist who eschewed the spotlight and most social activities. An avid sportsman despite a long history of physical problems, Pfister was likely happiest at his country home in Lake Five, surrounded by his beloved dogs.

Charles Pfister might have been a distant memory today, like other prominent men of his age, but he isn't. He still seems very much a part of the hotel that still bears his family name. The hotel, now known as the Pfister, is considered Milwaukee's most famously haunted building, as many believe that Charles Pfister is still there, delighting guests and watching over his father's dream hotel. Pfister sightings are too numerous to count, and all are reserved for the front, or "original," part of the hotel, with none in the addition built in the 1960s. Those who spot Pfister recognize him from the prominent oil painting of him that for many years overlooked the spectacular lobby. Pfister sightings happen most often on the grand staircase in the lobby, as well as in the Imperial Ballroom. Lucky ghost hunters sometimes spy Pfister walking the hallways of the eighth floor. It appears that Charles Pfister is still there, working to ensure that guests receive the premier service befitting his beloved hotel.

If it hadn't been for Major League Baseball, it is likely that the Pfister Hotel would not have reached the level of haunted fame it currently has. For years, baseball players have reported experiencing supernatural phenomena at the hotel. The list of players who have been affected enough to go on the record as having had a haunted experiences at the Pfister is long, playing for teams that include the Braves, Phillies, Reds, Marlins, Nationals and Giants, among others. Notably absent from this ever-growing list are players from the Milwaukee Brewers. If reports are to be believed, Brewers enjoy a comfortable stay at the Pfister, whereas players on these traveling teams have reported objects moving in their rooms, strange sounds, problems with electrical equipment, unexplained lights moving in rooms, voices and footsteps. Lest you think all of these ghostly encounters are from the distant past, think again, as a player for the Angels made national headlines in May 2016 when he reported being touched by what some call "the Pfister Ghost." The reports of the ghostly activity experienced by baseball players seem to be at odds with the genial sightings of Charles Pfister—or maybe not as much as it appears at first glance. Ever the loyal Milwaukee supporter, could all of these supernatural encounters be evidence that Mr. Pfister continues to root for the home team?

HISTORIC WHITE HOUSE TAVERN: 2900 SOUTH KINNICKINNIC AVENUE, MILWAUKEE

Built in 1891, the Queen Anne–style white clapboard tavern that stands at 2900 South Kinnickinnic Avenue is certainly one of Milwaukee's oldest, and possibly most haunted, taverns. Originally a Schlitz tavern operated by William Kneisler, the hardworking businessman quickly paid off the tied house debt, leaving the tavern owned by the family for 115 years.

In the early days, three generations of Kneislers lived in the second-floor apartments above the Bay View bar. While the busy White House Tavern prospered, quickly becoming an important social and political gathering place, in the rooms above, the Kneisler family met with a series of tragedies. The first to die in the apartment was the son, Alfred, after a painful bout of tuberculosis. Then little Norma was taken by an infection that resulted from an ice skating accident. Finally, Kneisler's mother, Wilhelmina, died in the family's rooms. The wakes for all three family members were held in the parlor of the apartment, as was customary. Some think there is reason to believe that the spirits of these lost Kneislers may be the source of the unusual activity reported in the tavern.

Employees report experiencing bottles moving behind the bar on their own, unexplained blasts of cold in the basements and eerily flickering lights in the attic. Bartenders have witnessed money levitating out of the cash register and have inexplicably encountered bar lamps crammed with glassware when opening the bar at the start of a shift. Much of this mischief seems to be done by an unseen hand, but there is an apparition that makes herself known to employees and patrons. Through the years, there have been countless sighting of Wilhelmina walking the hallway of White House. Those who've seen her say she is wearing a long, black, trained wedding dress, which they can hear *swish* and *crinkle* as she glides past them. Black wedding dresses were common for practical women of her era, and a photo of her wearing this dress can be seen in the vicinity of her sightings. Those who seek her out say that she is often found lingering in the area outside the bathroom.

While the bar is no longer owned by the Kneisler family, the new owner is no stranger to supernatural occurrences there. Bar manager Matthew Langoehr recounted to a local reporter an incident where he was sleeping in the apartment above the bar and was roused from a sound sleep at 2:00 a.m. by a loud knock at the door. When Langoehr, accompanied by his barking dog, who was also awakened by the knock, opened the door, he found no one there. In a separate interview, Sean Raphaelli, bar owner since 2005, told of a time he distinctly heard a little girl call out, "Mommy, mommy, let me in," at a time he was certain no one was present.

The Bay View landmark allows tavern-goers to step back into time. The floorboard are those trod on by generations of visitors, and it still has its original, well-polished bar, as well as, perhaps, some of its original occupants.

A COLLECTION OF TIDBITS ON MILWAUKEE'S MOST WELL-KNOWN HAUNTINGS

A celebrated Wisconsin folklorist once declared that Wisconsin had the most ghosts per square mile of any state. If his assertion is to be believed, these locations have certainly helped the Badger State earn that status.

Journal Sentinel Building: 333 West State Street, Milwaukee

When the Journal Sentinel Building at 333 West State Street opened in 1924, the Art Deco–style lobby was a bustle of customers purchasing classified advertising and taking care of their other daily business with the newspaper. Busy clerks lined the circular counter, speedily helping one customer after another, always rushing to ensure that needed additions were made before the paper went to press.

During an especially busy day in the lobby, a clerk very suddenly collapsed and died while in the process of working with a customer who was trying to place an ad in the paper. His abrupt death stunned not only those around him but himself as well—so much so, in fact, that it is said his spirit still remains in the lobby, busily trying to assist customers. Today, when an unexpected cold breeze is felt or an unexpected shadow passes in the lobby, it is acknowledged as the hardworking clerk of yesteryear, still on the job.

Former Offices of the Valentine Blatz Brewing Company: 1120 North Broadway

Located at 1120 North Broadway, this Romanesque–style building is now part of the Milwaukee School of Engineering's campus. Valentin Blatz, the innovative beer baron best known for creating Milwaukee's first individually bottled beers, made the building his brewery's headquarters in 1890.

A multimillionaire upon his death in 1894, Blatz was a notorious workhorse who eschewed outward signs of wealth and status. Leaving school at age fourteen to begin his career as a brewer, he tirelessly worked each day to develop his business. It is hardly unexpected when a man as devoted to his work as Val Blatz was refuses to let an inconvenience like death prevent him from coming into the office to get some work done.

An external view of the Blatz business office, now owned by MSOE. *Author's collection.*

Very shortly after his death, it was believed that his spirit returned to the office and remained, carefully watching the progress of his brewery. His contemporaries claimed that they could sense his presence in his former office and in meeting rooms. Others said they would occasionally smell his unique tobacco blend in the air. The belief that he was still there persisted even after the building was acquired by MSOE in 1989. Curious employees, determined to solve the mystery of the unusual happenings in the building, decided to host a séance there on Halloween in 1990.

The employees, with the help of a Milwaukee-based parapsychologist, did connect with a few spirits that night, although neither was Valentin Blatz. During the séance, the group made contact with Victor, a man they believed should have left the building sometime around 1933. The spirit seemed anxious to the group and was reportedly very concerned with money and other financial business. An elusive female spirit was sensed by the group, yet they could not communicate with her. During the séance, the participants reported "strange breezes" in the room that ceased when the session was complete. The experience did not rule out the possibility that Blatz remains, dutifully tending to his business, unfettered by those who try to interrupt his work.

The Shorecrest Hotel: 1962 North Prospect Avenue, Milwaukee

The Shorecrest Hotel, an Art Deco charmer located on Milwaukee's Eastside, is best known as the former hangout of notorious mob boss Frank Balistrieri. As the building's onetime owner, Frankie Bal, as he was sometimes called, was the undisputed king of the castle. Taking the eighth floor of the 116-unit building as his residence, he was often seen in the street-level restaurant in the building, then known as Snug's. The boss held court in the restaurant and was known to conduct business from a red telephone at his table whenever he was in the restaurant. A known hangout for mobsters and their molls, the place retains it aura of dangerous glamour even after all these years.

The tough guys and dirty dealers of yesteryear are gone now, but more than just the snappy décor remains. It is said that those who remain in the bar until closing time will hear the baby grand piano in the lobby of the former hotel being played. The unseen pianist softly plays, and then suddenly the music seems to drift away. The player is still known to tickle the ivories for lucky late-night guests to this day.

The Skylight Theater: 158 North Broadway #400, Milwaukee

Clair Richardson (1921–1980) was the famously flamboyant visionary who founded the Skylight Opera Theater in 1959. The former PR man was known for his theatrical dress and manner, but he is also remembered for the impact he had on the cultural development of Milwaukee. In addition to founding the Skylight Opera, he also worked to help develop the Milwaukee Repertory Theater, Milwaukee Symphony Orchestra and the Bel Canto Chorus. After running the Skylight Opera for twenty-one years, Richardson died during open-heart surgery. Richardson's pride, now known as the Skylight Music Theater, operates out of the Cabot Theater in the Historic Third Ward. Richardson appears to be as involved in the theater today as he was during his life. At his insistence, his ashes are being kept in an urn beneath the stage, so (as he explained) future decisions "would be made over his dead body." The urn, nestled on a shelf with a number of his belongings, is always ready for show time. It is reported that among the other duties of the stage manager, he is to make sure there is always a spotlight shining on the ashes. This became part of the official duties when it was discovered that a failure to ensure that Clair remained lit resulted in a number of unexplained technical problems, which were always resolved by making sure that the urn was in the spotlight. Richardson has also been known to wreak technical difficulties on performances that do not suit his taste.

GHASTLY PUBLIC SPACES

THEY GATHER WHERE WE GATHER

When bound to the earthly realm, it would appear that some spirits long to communicate with the living. There are those that reach out from beyond the dead to warn us of danger, while others need our help to rectify past events and some simply want their presences and stories known. Regardless of the reasons the restless souls linger, those that dwell in public spaces are much more likely to make the connections they crave with the mortal plane. This collection of stories chronicles a few noteworthy Milwaukee entities that remain in some of the city's most traveled areas.

THE FINAL COMMUTE: THE KINNICKINNIC RIVER BRIDGE, WISCONSIN HIGHWAY ROUTE 32

The morning of February 4, 1895, was a bitterly cold one. At fifteen degrees below zero, few had any interest in stepping outside. Nevertheless, morning commuters bundled up against the biting winds and frigid air to begin their workday. A small crowd gathered at the streetcar stop, waiting for Car 145 to come by and collect them, as it did every morning. The streetcar operator, James Kennedy, nodded to each of the passengers as he or she boarded, his face obscured by a heavy scarf and his eyes revealing the weariness he felt as he braced himself against the arctic blasts of wind. The twelve passengers sat close together, enduring their icy commute and eager to get back indoors.

The forty-two-year-old Kennedy navigated the car over the slick rails, focused more on his frozen toes and wind-chapped knuckles than the route. As the car approached the Kinnickinnic River Bridge, Kennedy realized, too late, that the drawbridge was open. The bridge operator frantically rang the bell, filling the frozen air with the sound of the alarm, as a tugboat in the water below looked on in horror. The motorman depressed the brake with all this might, but the streetcar skidded off the ice-covered rails and into the partially frozen river.

Large chunks of ice prevented the car from sinking the full eighteen feet to the bottom of the river. The men in the tug, there to break up ice on the river in order to allow larger boats to pass, rushed to rescue the passengers. Kennedy survived the wreck, but noticing that two passengers were not accounted for, he stayed with the car, diving into the submerged car again and again to search for two missing women. Ultimately, the dangerously cold water was too much for the motorman to endure, and he succumbed to the icy grip of the river. With him were his two trapped passengers, twenty-six-year-old kindergarten teacher Antoinette Ehlman and thirty-three-year-old Nation Knitting Works employee Katie Schmidkunz.

A view from the bridge overlooking what Milwaukeeans affectionately call the KK River. *Photo by author.*

Those frozen, soaked bodies were taken from the river that day, but some are convinced that the spirits of commuters never left the site of that awful accident. Perhaps this explains the strange mists seen at the mouth of the bridge? Is it Kennedy, cautioning motorists of the danger ahead? Or could it be all three souls, taken so unexpectedly they remain there, lost and unsure how to move on? Walk across the bridge and you may feel a chill as a creeping fog envelops you at the site of this tragedy.

The Fairview and the Firefighters: Milwaukee Engine House 35, 100 North 64th Street

When a final resting place for the dead is disturbed, there can be supernatural consequences. The movement of entombed bodies could be the source of the odd things that occur at Milwaukee Engine House 35 on Milwaukee's Westside. Built in 1998, the modern building does not look like a place restless spirits would appear, and yet a number of area firefighters believe that the engine house, nicknamed the "Crypt Keeper," is rife with supernatural activity. Employees of the firehouse believe that the source of the strange happenings is paranormal because the building was erected on the former site of the Fairview Mausoleum. The now demolished crypt was an imposing, black granite building that housed 999 of the dearly departed and included an on-site crematorium and chapel.

Built in 1912, the ominous-looking Neoclassical building frightened generations of kids in the neighborhood. The mausoleum was creepy from the onset, and when financial problems led the property to fall into disrepair, the structure began to look outright sinister. The unkempt landscaping and crumbling façade of the mausoleum increased the Fairview's spooky reputation. Finally, in 1996, the city took over the decaying building and began relocating the entombed residents to Graceland Cemetery. By 1997, all the dead had been removed and laid to rest, but not in another mausoleum; instead, they were interred in the ground in Section 11 of the cemetery. Today, visitors can see a pair of large stone pillars from the former Fairview Mausoleum rising from the lawn in the graveyard at Graceland, marking the burial site of the mausoleum's former inhabitants. The most noteworthy of these former Fairview dwellers is Captain Edward Gifford Crosby, along with his wife and daughter. The family were passengers on the infamous RMS *Titanic*; the women fled the sinking ship in a lifeboat and survived, but

An advertising postcard for the now defunct Fairview Mausoleum. *CardCow.*

the captain succumbed to the icy waters. His body was recovered from the ocean, cremated and returned to Milwaukee to rest at the Fairview. In later years, when his wife and daughter passed from the earthly realm, they joined Captain Crosby in the mausoleum.

It could be suggested that some of the dead who were relocated weren't interested in finding a new final resting place. Unusual events on the property where the Fairview once stood give many reason to believe that spirits linger on the land. Firefighters on all shifts have reported the sounds of footsteps without a source in the halls of the engine house. Mischievous spirits have also been known to throw pots and pans in the empty kitchen. Bolder spirits in the house have interacted with the employees. Two firefighters sitting on either side of a floor lamp witnessed the plug of the lamp fly from the outlet in the wall, plunging the room in darkness. Neither of the witnesses could explain how the plug was forcefully removed from the outlet without being touched. Another nightshift employee sleeping in the basement of the engine house woke to the feeling of being violently held down. Wrestling with the unseen entity, the physically powerful fireman was eventually able to free himself from the invisible grasp of the intruder. The next morning, he discovered bruises on his torso in the exact places he felt he was held down. Another night shift employee awoke to see an apparition next to his bed.

A view of the new firehouse, built in 1998. *Photo by author.*

The spirit—dressed in a bowler hat, vest and woolen pants—disappeared without a trace when the fireman turned to look at him.

Is Captain Crosby one of the spirits that remain at the site of the former mausoleum? Some think he might be. Since opening, the station has had a number of reports of the bathroom water faucet turning on by itself in the middle of the night. When this occurs, the tap is always fully opened and the water always frigidly cold. Do these torrents of icy water, mimicking the deluge of bitterly cold ocean water that flooded the ill-fated *Titanic*, point to his presence in the engine house? Is he the mysterious man in the bowler hat? His body was found days after the sinking wearing a green tweed suit, with his wallet and other personal effects still on him. While Crosby was found hatless, bowler hats were a popular fashion on the boat, particularly in the first-class cabins the captain frequented.

Many are intrigued by the thought of the long-dead *Titanic* casualty residing in the firehouse, but not all firefighters assigned to the house accept that the house is haunted. Some reject the existence of the supernatural and shrug off the unexplained activities in the building. Those with firsthand experience with these events feel differently. Although the firefighters do not agree about the presence of spirits in the house, they all agree that strange occurrences at Engine House 35 have never interfered with their service to the community.

PERILOUS PARKS

Lake Park is not the only one of Milwaukee's 136 parks where people have experienced supernatural phenomena. Among the most commonly cited public grounds for experiencing the otherworldly are Grant Park and Whitnall Park. Visitors flock to both of the popular parks to enjoy the natural beauty of the grounds, but there are those who report seeing far more than they ever expected, or hoped, to encounter during a fun outing to the park.

Grant Park: Seven Bridges Trail, South Milwaukee

Entering Grant Park's Seven Bridges trail, walkers are welcomed by a sign reading, "Enter this wild wood and view the haunts of nature." If the rumors are to be believed, far more than nature haunts these mystical trails. Developed in the early 1900s by Frederick C. Wulff, the trail became the grand two-mile ramble it is today during the 1930s, when a WPA project allowed for the construction of the lannon stone paths, staircases and the much-celebrated seven bridges that tie the paths together. The park, nestled next to the shore of Lake Michigan, has the feeling of a dense, remote forest despite being surrounded by a well-populated residential neighborhood. In the daytime, the trail is filled with nature enthusiasts, joggers and families strolling with baby carriages. At night, the trail belongs to the spirits that have made Seven Bridges Trail their home.

Exactly what haunts these secluded trails is unknown. Some say the area is haunted by those who have been murdered on these lonely pathways, their spirits seeking to make a connection to the living. Others claim that the supernatural activity comes from those who have chosen to end their lives in these woods. Many believe that a number of those suicides occurred right at the covered bridge entrance to the trail. A few have claimed that a ghostly woman, searching for her children, is a source of the paranormal energy that charges this area at night.

While the reason behind the haunting remains debated by those exploring the trail, there are a few common experiences reported by those who have dared to venture on the trail after dark. Seekers report seeing unexplained colored lights dancing in the woods. Many have seen a misty apparition on the covered bridge, sometimes coming up from other the bridge and other times suddenly appearing next to them as they cross the bridge over

The entryway that greets visitors at the head of a trail many believe to be haunted. *Author's collection*.

One of the forty carved heads that can be found in Grant Park. *Photo by author*.

the ravine. Those on the unpaved portion of the trail closer to the beach have spotted a glowing woman, clad in white, seeking children who long ago drowned in Lake Michigan's cold depths.

Nocturnal walkers near the stone bench have reported hearing terrified screams from deep in the empty woods. Perhaps they are the screams of those murdered long ago in the park, warning the walkers of danger that lies ahead? Most frighteningly, those undeterred by the specters and ghostly screams continue along the deserted paths have heard disembodied footsteps walking toward them, accompanied by heavy breathing. As the footstep grow nearer, and the breathing begins thundering in their ears, it suddenly passes over them, leaving a feeling of fear and dread in its wake.

Those who wish to walk the Seven Bridges trail in the moonlight should note that Grant Park closes at 10:00 p.m. and is regularly patrolled by the police.

Whitnall Park: 5879 South 92nd Street, Franklin

With a golf course, nature center and botanical gardens, Whitnall Park is Milwaukee's largest and most well-appointed public park. The sprawling 627-acre park, named for former County Parks commissioner Charles B. Whitnall, has one less well-advertised feature: its very own ghost.

Lacing through the park is a river way. In the center of its path is the sixteen-acre Whitnall Pond, which has a waterfall on its northern end. It is at that waterfall that a number of park visitors have experienced the apparition of a young mother in distress. The wispy, pale vision appears suddenly. Rather than fleeing from her uninvited guests, her footless form appears to float toward the park visitor. Above the roar of the waterfall, the crying of a baby can be heard. Some frightened witnesses have even heard her speak, claiming that she warns them to go away and leave her unseen baby alone. The protective mother then flees into the woods, toward her wailing infant, and disappears from sight. Are the woman and her child spirits that remain from the time the area was largely farmland? Has a long-forgotten accident rooted the pair in this picturesque area? Who they are and why they remain is as unknown as it is mysterious.

CREEPY CAMPUSES

Milwaukee's schools of higher education are filled with stories of specters haunting campuses. From the spirits of pesky dorm room dwellers determined to frighten residents to the ghosts of those forever connected to the buildings that were significant to them in life, it seems as if area schools are teeming with supernatural energy.

Concordia University of Wisconsin

Established in 1886, Concordia University of Wisconsin moved to its current location when it purchased its Mequon campus from the School Sisters of Norte Dame in 1982. This 1958 construction does not have the outward appearance of a place where restless souls dwell, but looks are often deceiving. Built by the Sisters as a convent and teacher training facility, campus legend says that some of the nuns were reluctant to leave the buildings when the campus was purchased by the university. Perhaps at least one of those unhappy nuns found a way to remain on the campus after the School Sisters of Norte Dame officially relocated. Current students report electrical disturbances, items moved by an unseen hand and specter sightings—all blamed on the troubled spirit the students have named "Sister Six Toes."

Students living in the Augsburg, Coburg and Katherine dormitories report odd occurrences they attribute to the supernatural. The Sister has been blamed for turning on faucets, televisions and lights. She is also known to move objects around the dorm rooms, keeping the students searching for their items. While it might be easy to dismiss these experiences as the result of students being careless, it is harder to explain away the late-night sightings of the Sister as her ghostly outline roams the area around the campus chapel at night.

It is said that the Sister is forever connected to the school because she passed from the earthly realm in the chapel. Now a favorite spot for her, those students brave enough to roam the hallways and staircases around the chapel may see her, her habit-clad outline silently making its way through the night, firmly rooted in the place she once loved.

Cardinal Stritch University

Established in 1937 by the Sisters of St. Francis Assisi, the school was moved to its current Northshore location in 1962. For many years, students have delighted in terrifying one another with creepy tales of the haunting of Clare Residence Hall. Campus lore suggests that in the early days of the school, ailing nuns living at CSU were moved to an infirmary in the basement of Clare Hall. Perhaps a few of the sick nuns died in the infirmary and their spirits continue to linger in Clare Hall.

Residents on the third floor of the Center wing have grappled for years with an unseen hand that tears posters and other room décor from walls and sends shelved objects tumbling to the floor. Generations of students living in 3C claim to have witnessed locked doors swing open without logical explanation. Students on the second floor of the West wing relate hearing sounds of someone running down the halls in the dead of the night. 2W dwellers state that when they open their dorm room doors to find the source of the noise, the running stops and the runner is unseen, only for the sounds to begin again once the investigator climbs back into bed. Students in all wings of the dorm have spotted a ghostly, habit-clad nun roaming the hallways at night, her name unknown and the meaning of sightings unclear. Regardless of the reasons she remains in Clare Hall, her otherworldly presence is felt throughout the building.

Marquette University

Long known as one of Milwaukee's most haunted locations, Marquette University's urban campus is bristling with paranormal activity. From ghosts that linger because of their connection to the school to those that were acquired as new building were added to the campus, the school is a hub for restless spirits.

STRAZ TOWER was a YMCA facility until 1993, when it was purchased by the university. The eighteen-story residence hall has a number of amenities, including a YMCA-era basement-level pool in what is now known as the Rex Plex. Among the dorm's 360 student residents is Whispering Willie, the building's most famous apparition. Willie, as the spirit of the young boy has been named, drowned in the pool many years ago. Late-night swimmers report suddenly seeing Willie swimming next to them as they complete their laps. The youngster appears in the lane with the swimmer, matching the

A Gothic-style doorway leading to Johnston Hall. *Author's collection*.

stride for a few strokes, and then disappears as suddenly as he appeared. Willie is also thought to be the source of dorm room shenanigans, reportedly responsible for blankets being pulled off sleeping students and lights turning on and off without human intervention.

Carpenter Tower, the Art Deco gem of the campus, was opened in 1930 under the name of Catholic Knights Insurance Society Hotel. Later known as Tower Hotel, this residence hall is known to have a young former hotel guest who has yet to check out. A young boy, thought to have perished in a fire in the hotel, has been seen looking out of the upper windows of the building. The boy's mournful stare to those below elicits more pity than fear in those who see him. Dubbed "Jeremy" by the students, his presence in a room is said to cause unplugged electronics to inexplicably turn on.

It's not just the residence halls where spirits lurk on the campus, identified as one of the ten most haunted colleges in the Midwest by Mysterious Heartland. Two theater-loving spirits also make their presence known at Marquette University. Helfaer Theater is supposedly haunted by the spirit of an art director who died in the studio. Visitors to the theater claim that he makes his presence known through banging and clanging noises coming from the catwalk. The Varsity Theater is said to be haunted by a helpful ghost that met a grim end. Rumor suggests that years ago, an unlucky projectionist working in the theater fell into an industrial fan and was sliced to bits. Today, the custodial crew credits him with helping lock up and turn out lights at the end of shifts.

The gorgeously ornamented, Gothic-styled Johnston Hall was completed in 1907, and the current Media Center was at one time Jesuit living quarters. Tragically, in August 1963, a priest fell off, or leaped to his death from, the fifth-floor balcony that faces Church of the Gesu. Those willing to venture to the fifth floor at night report a great deal of unexplained activity, from sounds of disembodied footfalls to doors opening and closing on their own. In the 1990s, a few ghost-hunting students representing the campus publication *Marquette Tribune* conducted a nocturnal investigation of the fifth floor of the building. The students documented the discovery of cold spots and strange noises, saw an unusual blue light and caught a shadowy figure on tape. All of this strengthened the assertions that the building is home to a restless spirit. Complicating all of this are the persistent rumors that Johnston Hall was built on Native American burial land, making it a cursed endeavor from the beginning.

The campus building with the most reported paranormal activity is certainly Humphrey Hall. The location of Children's Hospital from 1923

The entryway to the Varsity Theater in Holthusen Hall. *Author's collection.*

until 1988, the building had a fully equipped basement-level morgue when the University acquired it. While extensively remodeled in 2015, that has not stopped its tiniest residents from making themselves known. Small bands of ghostly children clad in hospital gowns are seen, and heard, all over the building. Giggling and playing games, these playful spirits have been caught on security cameras and observed disappearing into solid walls when curious spirit seekers have gotten too close to them. On the fifth floor of the building, there is an impish young girl who tries to draw the living into her endless game of hide-and-seek. The first floor is home to another former patient who loves playing with her ball in the hallways, her watchful eyes following the movements of those who venture into her play area.

Carroll University

Established in 1841, Carroll University is best known as Wisconsin's oldest institution of higher learning. Located in the center of the city of Waukesha, the campus spills into the surrounding residential neighborhood. Like the other schools, Carroll's campus has reports of supernatural activity. MacAllister Hall, originally built as the home of lumber magnate George Wilbur in 1895, is thought to be the school's most haunted building since it became a dormitory in 1948.

Donated to the school after Wilbur's death, the stately mansion served as a Civil War museum until it was remodeled and converted into student housing. Immediately after students took up residence in the converted home, unusual things began to occur. Dorm dwellers reported doors opening and closing on their own. More unnerving were the reports of disembodied voices and moans coming from the hallways and seemingly between the walls.

Generations of MacAllister residents have caught sight of Mr. and Mrs. Wilbur, in formal attire, walking through walls as if oblivious to the changes made to the home's floorplan in the years after their deaths. A number of students claim to have been awakened and playfully touched by the translucent figure of a man wearing an overcoat. It is thought that this nocturnal visitor is Ray Wilber, son of George Wilbur and a vice-president in his father's lumber business, a position he held until his death in 1938. Paranormal activity seems to have reached a fevered pitch in the 1970s, when a male student woke from a deep sleep with unexplained bloodied scratches on his chest that he was certain were supernatural in origin.

In 2010, a group of students conducted a paranormal investigation of the building, live-streaming their Ouija board session and other tests to the campus. During the session, their camera died despite being fully charged. Participants in the search also recorded doors slamming on their own, lights turning themselves on and off and cold spots in doorways. Now used as an office for campus staff, the building retains its ghoulish reputation.

SHUDDERSOME CEMETERIES

Graveyards are inherently scary; they are the earthly reminder that our time in this realm is limited. These gateways to the other world so frighten us that we've developed an exhaustive number of rituals and superstitions for how people should interact with burial grounds. We hold our breath when we pass a cemetery to prevent a restless spirit from entering us and are careful to tuck our thumbs into our fists to prolong the lives of our parents. Counting the cars in a funeral procession will doom the counter to a certain death in the number of days equal to the number of cars in the procession. Leaving a grave open overnight is a sure way to summon the grim reaper, just as being the first to leave a funeral will invite death to take one of your family members next. These practices persist because the uncertainty of what happens after this life frightens us, and no place better reminds us of our mortality than the final resting places for our physical bodies.

La Belle Cemetery, Oconomowoc

Established in 1851, La Belle Cemetery expanded into donated land in 1864 to meet the needs of the growing community. On the shores of Fowler Lake, this graveyard is the final resting place of a number of notable former residents, including John Rockwell, popularly considered the "father of Oconomowoc."

In the bucolic cemetery, hiding in plain sight, is a flurry of paranormal activity. The focal point of this unearthly activity appears to be the final resting place of the Nathusias family. The plot's now famous stone monument, depicting a nearly life-size young woman in mourning in front of a rugged, rough-hewn cross twice her size, commands attention.

The often-visited Nathusias family plot at La Belle Cemetery. *Author's collection.*

A closer view of the stone girl who has attracted so many visitors. *Author's collection.*

Legends swirl around the sorrowful-looking stone girl. Over the years, many have claimed that the statue cries tears of blood, with a few claiming that blood also seeps from her lightly clasped stone hands. Some have even claimed to see the statue freeing herself from her base and walking toward Fowler Lake. The most compelling story told about this statue is the nocturnal company she is said to keep. A young girl is said to linger at the monument after dusk. When the luminescent apparition of the girl is spotted by the stone monument, nighttime visitors know that an eerie scene is about to take place. As the visitors approach the ghostly girl, just as generations before them have, she flees toward the lake, flinging herself into the water, where she appears to drown. The reason for this scene remains a mystery, as there are no young girls buried in the family plot and no known drownings connected to that part of Fowler Lake's shoreline.

Devoted visitors to the monument are known to leave offering for the statue. Some bring live flowers to pair with the stone ones she holds in her arms. Others leave coins or trinkets in her cupped hands. Schoolyard tales often repeated by children of the community warn of blindness and other calamities that are certain to befall anyone who dares to steal an offering made to the forever-mourning stone girl. Pass through the gates of La Belle Cemetery to meet her yourself, if you dare.

Tabernacle Cemetery, Delafield Township

Rural Tabernacle Cemetery has been the source of supernatural stories for more than one hundred years. It began in 1842 as the final resting place for the congregants of the now defunct First Welsh Congregational Church of Delafield. Now a private cemetery, the much talked-about graveyard is off-limits to visitors.

Legend has it that the first soul to be buried there was a young farm boy who accidentally hanged himself in a barn while doing chores. Deeply distraught over the unexpected loss of the boy, the owner of the barn boldly painted the name of the boy on the side of his barn for all to see in commemoration of the loss. The farmer's public mourning, revealed in giant letters on a building overlooking the young boy's grave, broke the hearts of all who saw it. Some say that it is this remembrance that keeps the boy's spirit connected to the area. Restless in death, the boy is thought to be the source of mysterious bright lights that appear in the graveyard at night. There is no known source of this nocturnal light show, and reports of these sightings predate the invention of the lightbulb.

If the farm boy does still linger in the yard, ghost hunters say he is not alone. Often seen by startled motorists, the apparition of a short, stout, middle-aged man lingers near the Tabernacle Cemetery sign on Bryn Drive. Tales swirl around the source of this specter, but the most often-retold version of the tale is that the man was the victim of a fatal car accident. Whether his presence is meant to serve as a sign of caution to drivers of the lonely road or is frightening enough to be the cause of another accident is uncertain.

Since the 1840s, the curious have come to Tabernacle to experience for themselves these supernatural happenings. While no reasonable explanation has ever been given for the otherworldly events witnessed by generations, there are two reported phenomena whose source is easy to trace. Modern ghost hunters often report a "feeling of being watched" while on the grounds, and some report that late-night visitors are chased off the property by a dark truck with exceptionally bright lights. These actions are not the work of spirits, but rather the employee hired, in part, to prevent trespassing on these private grounds. Long plagued by vandals, the grounds are now closed—at least to the living.

Calvary Cemetery, Milwaukee

Consecrated on the spiritually significant All Saints' Day in 1857, the current Calvary Cemetery is the final resting place of an estimated seventy thousand souls. Owned by the Archdiocese of Milwaukee, the site is thought to be the oldest existing Roman Catholic cemetery in Milwaukee. Found among the rows of tombstones are the monuments to those lost in the tragic Newhall House fire and the wreck of the *Lady Elgin*. While boasting a less extensive roll of former Milwaukee power brokers than its crosstown companion, the Forest Home Cemetery, the Calvary is not without its share of notables, including the celebrated first white settler and first mayor, Solomon Juneau.

In a less showy plot, at the base of Jesuit Hill, in the shadow of the Calvary Cemetery Chapel, lies another historically significant Milwaukeean, P. Walter H. Halloran. Those interested in occultism, as well as fans of the 1973 horror classic *The Exorcist*, likely recognize his name. Father Halloran, one of the three priests who participated in the real-life exorcism on which the horror classic is based, was laid to rest at Calvary Cemetery upon his death in 2005. A lifelong midwesterner, this former Marquette University instructor spent his retirement years at St. Camillus Retirement Community.

Halloran was only twenty-seven years old at the time he assisted Reverends Bowdern and Van Roos in the 1949 exorcism of Roland Doe, and the notoriety of the famous case followed him for the remainder of his life. He was chosen to assist in the rites largely because a young, strong man was needed to restrain the fourteen-year-old St. Louis boy clergy identified as being possessed by the devil. By the time Halloran joined the group, it had already been determined that an evil entity had invaded the boy's body. The source of the problem, the reverends concluded, was that the boy's aunt had introduced him to Ouija board use. Shortly after her death, strange things began happening in the house. The family reported unusual noises in the home and witnessed objects flying through the air. Intervention by the holy men seemed to exacerbate the situation, resulting in increased activity in the home and disturbing behavior from the boy.

The reverends witnessed Roland Doe succumb to fits of cursing and seemingly uncontrolled bouts of urinating and vomiting. When talking with the boy, they observed how his voice changed to a low, demonic snarl and noted that the boy was repelled by religious relics. Initially, the men attempted the exorcism on their own, with disastrous results. During the exorcism, the men claim that Doe's bed shook violently and objects flew around the room. At a critical point in the ceremony, the boy was able to loosen his arm restraints, rip a bed coil from the mattress and stab one of the reverends in the arm, ending the rite abruptly.

After a failed attempt to rid Roland Doe of the demon on their own, the men had Halloran join them in March 1949. Halloran participated in three rites between March 16 and April 18, 1949. The final exorcism took place in a psychiatric unit at the Alexian Brothers Hospital in St. Louis.

Chapel Hill, where many Jesuit graves at the Calvary Cemetery are located. *Author's collection.*

Notable Jesuit grave markers at the peak of Chapel Hill. *Author's collection.*

In the days leading up to the final ritual, physical signs appeared on the boy's body, including scratches and streaks on his skin that seemed to come from inside his body. The men also witnessed the word *hell*, written in deep scratches, surface on the boy's skin. So violent were the rites that Halloran ended up with a broken nose after one of the rituals. After the final ritual, it was believed that the demon had been vanquished, and Roland Doe was free of possession.

Much controversy, both inside and outside the church, resulted from the events of 1949. For his part, Halloran never definitely responded to questions about the validity of the possession, claiming that he lacked the expertise to make the judgement. Far less uncertain was Bowdern, whose diaries of the events were the source material for the blockbuster film. Until his death, he remained steadfast to the idea that he and the other holy men battled the devil in 1949.

In the years after the exorcism, Halloran went on to serve with valor in the Vietnam War, earning two Bronze Stars. After returning to civilian life, the cleric taught at a number of midwestern universities.

While always remembered for the events of 1949, it is clear his accomplishments went well beyond those strange events in St. Louis.

Forest Home Cemetery, Milwaukee

Milwaukee's most celebrated cemetery is, undoubtedly, Forest Home Cemetery. Established by the congregation of St. Paul's Episcopal Church, located in Yankee Hill, this garden cemetery saw its first burial in 1850. Now covering a sprawling two hundred acres, this graveyard is listed in the National Register of Historic Places. Politicians, beer barons, industrialists and a significant portion of Milwaukee's elite from previous eras have found their home in this restful oasis.

Perhaps it is this notoriety that discourages the kind of hauntings that seem to take place in remote cemeteries. Today, Forest Home Cemetery is a popular tourist spot, filled with historical tours, costumed reenactors and artists capturing pieces of Milwaukee's past on film and canvas. Maybe all of this activity causes restless spirits to be elusive, or at least harder to recognize.

Those who come to Forest Home to seek supernatural experiences avoid the well-visited sites of war heroes and history makers and instead gravitate to the north side of the grounds. Away from the Hall of History and closer

A view of the grounds of the famous Forest Home Cemetery. *Author's collection.*

The mausoleum of beer baron Valentin Blatz inside Forest Home Cemetery. *Author's collection.*

to the crematorium, those sensitive to the spiritual world describe some disturbing things as they roam these hallowed grounds. Visitors recount eerie feelings in this area, accompanied by acute fearfulness, even in the daytime and while being accompanied by others. While walking in Sections 62 and 64, visitors have encountered cold spots, and some have even told of being touched by an unseen hand in this area. Most disturbingly, a number of have described experiencing horrible visions in the north side of the yard. The visions include images of splintered coffins and shredded corpses. These nightmare-inducing scenes are sometimes accompanied by the sounds of a woman crying. The explanation for this experience is unknown, but the sensitive say that the area causes physical illness, reporting bouts of headaches, blurred visions, bloodshot eyes and nausea, all of which vanish once the person leaves the area.

What lingers in the Forest Home Cemetery that causes these otherworldly experiences remains a mystery that may be best pondered as you roam the winding roads of the grounds. Visitors are welcome from sunrise to sunset, and several self-guided tours of the grounds are available to aid the curious in finding their favorites from Milwaukee's past.

ECHOES OF THE PAST

Have you ever felt a sudden, unexplained feeling of dread cross over you? Have you walked into a room and experienced a sudden need to flee? When we have these experiences, we dismiss them as our being tired or preoccupied by the stress of daily life—anything but a supernatural experience. Perhaps we dismiss these feelings too easily. It could be that sudden headache or sense of unease you feel is an echo from the past. The feeling could derive from something or someone you can't see, that history may have forgotten, but is still with us and making itself known.

THE FIFTEENTH STREET MISERY:
AREA OF NORTH 15TH AND WEST WALNUT STREETS

On April 1, 1889, a tragedy occurred on what is now the Northside of Milwaukee. The events of that evening were so horrible that it seems as if the people involved in the living nightmare that occurred on what was then known as Fifteenth Street remain in this realm, forever tied to the land.

Margaret Kinlein was a Bavarian immigrant who arrived in Milwaukee with her carpenter husband in the 1880s. The pair worked hard and purchased a small, two-story wooden framed home in the area of 15th and Walnut Streets. The couple occupied the first floor and had tenants renting the second floor of the home. In time, their family grew, and by 1888, the pair had three sons: six-year-old John, four-year-old George and two-year-old

Frank. The happy family was active in their church and the community, and they were well liked and content with the life they had built in Milwaukee.

In the early days of January 1889, Mr. Kinlein was suddenly seized by uncontrollable coughing spells. They soon realized that he was not battling a winter cold, but rather what at the time was known as "quick acting consumption." By January 9, carpenter Kinlein, the family's sole breadwinner, was dead.

The widowed Margaret was stunned at the unforeseen loss of her husband and fell into a deep despair. Neighbors began to whisper about her behavior, noting her "fits of melancholia" and her lack of stoicism in the face of the unexpected loss. By late March, it appeared that the woman had become entirely unraveled, spending most of her days lamenting over what would happen to her and her young boys now that she no longer had a husband to provide for them. As the month closed, Margaret began to talk obsessively about suicide. Things in the house became so frightening that the twelve-year-old live-in servant girl, Lena Ebert, fled the home. Six-year-old John went after the girl, begging her to stay, but she refused. Margaret Kinlein no longer seemed sane, and Lena feared that if she remained in the home, harm would come to her. As night fell, Mrs. Kinlein gathered her children indoors and readied them for bed.

In the early hours the next morning, the second-floor tenants awoke to smoke filling their rooms. The renting Jung family acted quickly, managing to flee the home while sending their son to sound the fire alarm. Shortly after 2:00 a.m., the fire department arrived. The Jung family assumed that the Kinleins had already escaped the home, as they pounded on the doors and windows of the home but had gotten no response. Once the firefighters managed to force open the door of the home, they soon discovered the horrible truth about the blaze.

In a room tightly sealed, the men found the family lying together in one bed. It was clear that the blaze started under the bed. Margaret Kinlein was a truly horrifying sight; the woman's body had burned so badly she no longer had any hair, and her feet had completed burned away. Next to her were the charred bodies of John and George. Later, the body of young Frank was found in the basement. His body had burned so badly that it burned through the floor of the bedroom and fell to the basement floor below. The cause of the tragedy was not a mystery. It was very clear that the widow had put the children in bed with her and started a fire beneath the bed.

It is not known exactly how the mother and her children died. Those who loved the family during happier times hoped that they succumbed to the

Vintage photograph of an unknown Milwaukee toddler. *Author's collection.*

smoke long before the flames reached their bodies. The medical examiner, after viewing the bodies, suggested the family may have been drugged, as he felt it would be too difficult to overcome the instinct to escape once the smoke made breathing impossible. The horrified neighbors of the Kinleins prayed that he was right.

The home is long gone now. In its place is a fenced-in grassy lot, but the land might not be as vacant as it initially appears. Those walking past the plot of land feel an unexpected sense of dread pass over them as they pass along the sidewalk. The sensitive experience a tightness in the chest, and fear begins to gnaw at the pit of the stomach. Are they feeling the same fear the young boys felt their last night on earth? Was the terror of that final evening so powerful the area is forever marked with it, or do the spirits of the brothers linger in the area, warning the innocent to stay away? The exact cause of the phenomena is unknown, but it is clear that the land has been permanently marked by the terror of the early morning hours on April 1, 1889.

THE RIVERSIDE STROLL: PLEASANT VALLEY PARK, MILWAUKEE RIVER

Four young men were enjoying a summer's day excursion on the Milwaukee River in late August 1893. As the group of friends rowed through Pleasant Valley Park, one of them spotted something odd it the water. The curious young men debated about what it could be as they maneuvered their rowboat closer to the strange object bobbing in the current in the middle of the river. As they got closer to the object, the boat filled with a sense of dread. They had not found a mysterious treasure—they had found the body of woman, tied tightly to a heavy weight. The boys quickly alerted the authorities.

The police had some difficulty removing the body from the river, as it was fastened to a nearly sixty-pound stone. When the ropes that bound the woman's arms to her torso and the weight to her midsection were removed, the police made a search of the body. Nothing was found on the body to help the police identify the water-logged corpse, but the woman was well dressed, wearing expensive, fashionable clothing and a heavy gold ring. This dark-haired woman estimated to be about thirty years old had to have been someone's wife, they reasoned, as she appeared to be well taken care of. Yet no one had reported a missing person who matched the description of the woman, and no one came forward after a description of the body was published in the newspaper. The police thought that the circumstances screamed of foul play: a well-dressed woman no one had claimed was found in the river with her arms bound and secured to a sixty-pound weight indicated murder to the investigators. The coroner saw things differently and declared the body a suicide, despite the protests that she did not appear to be a woman who could carry a sixty-pound weight and because it was not possible for her to bind her own arms. The coroner was unmoved, and the death continued to be marked as a suicide.

The coroner may have had the last word in the case if the scene did not repeat itself the very next day. A pair of sporting gentlemen were rowing through the park and discovered the body of a young girl who was bound and weighed down in a similar fashion. The little girl was also expensively dressed and appeared to be well cared for. Because of their clothing, the location where the bodies were discovered and the way they were tied and anchored, the police assumed that the pair were mother and daughter. The coroner persisted, suggesting the woman had killed her daughter and then herself, but the police didn't think this was a likely scenario. Neither did the public, and the police started to receive tips about strange activity on the river a few days earlier. They began their investigation, and within a day, the police had the murderer in custody.

It took little effort for the police to get a full confession from Gustave Scharff. The mother and daughter pulled from the river, identified as Ollie and Gracie King, were well acquainted with their murderer. The man was the woman's paramour, and six-year-old Gracie was her child by a previous relationship. Ollie King's life had not been easy; her mother died when she was young, and she was sent to live with distant relatives. When she and her father were reunited, he had married another woman who was expecting a child, and Ollie was not welcomed to join his new household. She was sent to be a live-in servant at a Milwaukee-area home and lived such a miserable existence that she contemplated suicide. Young and desperate, she met an older man who said he would help her, and in a short time, she was in the unenviable position of being a pregnant girl without a family or husband.

Ollie persevered and made her living working in sporting houses, leaving young Gracie in the care of others. It was during that time she met the man who would become her murderer. Scharff frequented the type of establishments where Ollie made her living, and soon they began to see each other romantically. They even shared living quarters for a time. Scharff may have been happy with the arrangement, but the women in his life certainly were not. When Sharff's mother and aunt discovered who he was keeping company with, they demanded he end the relationship. At roughly the same time, Ollie discovered she was pregnant and demanded he marry her. His family wanted Ollie gone, and Scharff's attempts to end the relationship with the woman were unsuccessfully; she wasn't going anywhere. Gustave Scharff felt trapped and did not know how to how to appease all the women in his life. He began to hatch a plan.

The man offered to take Ollie on an outing, suggesting she should bring her daughter. While he initially promised the pair a trip to Chicago, they ended up taking a stroll through Pleasant Valley Park. Reclining in the grass next to the riverbed in the park, the couple talked as young Gracie napped a few feet away. Without warning, Scharff set upon the woman, his hands wrapped tightly around her neck and squeezing her windpipe closed. The startled and confused woman fought back, but Scharff persisted, confessing that he strangled his pregnant lover for ten minutes before he was certain she was dead and released his hold. He then went over to the sleeping child and placed his murderous hands on her throat, repeating the evil deed.

With the mother and child dead, the man rented a boat to dispose of the bodies in the Milwaukee River. His terrible secret did not remain unknown for long. Justice moved quickly, and within the week the confessed murderer was sentenced to jail time and hard labor for the rest of his life.

While Ollie and Gracie got the justice those following the case wanted for the pair, they do not rest peacefully in the Forest Home Cemetery, where the mother and child are buried. The well-dressed pair, both in the fashionably cut black frocks, can still be seen walking hand in hand on the shoreline on that stretch of the Milwaukee River. Perhaps it was the utter surprise of their deaths that keeps the pair there, or maybe it is a sign of Ollie's strength and defiance, refusing to let anyone dispose of her. Whatever the reason for their presence, the two are a sight to behold.

FOR THE LOVE OF DRINK: GROUNDS OF MILWAUKEE SOLDIERS HOME

English-born W.G. Wilkinson fought for the Union in the early days of the Civil War. Once discharged, he decided to make the battle-torn country his permanent home. It was a difficult life for Wilkinson: he had no family here, his skills as a musician did not provide many financial opportunities in the midst of a war and an illness left him with an amputated leg. But all of those obstacles seemed insignificant once he met Maggie. The young German immigrant was beautiful, known for her locks of flowing dark hair, and was a very hard worker with a reputation as an excellent housekeeper. Wilkinson thought this lovely girl was perfect for him, and after a few months of courting, she agreed and consented to marry him.

By 1880, the pair had three daughters—ages three and two years and four months—and were living in a row of cottages on the National Soldiers Home grounds. The man's cornet skills had helped him land a job as the leader of the Home Band on the grounds. He was well liked by the men in the band he led, and the family made enough money, with the help of some additional income from boarders, for Mrs. Wilkinson to avoid taking work outside the home. While observers thought the forty-year-old bandleader had a happy life with his lovely young bride and three little girls, the truth was that their domestic life was much darker. Wilkinson had a love of whiskey that was tearing the family apart.

His binge drinking caused his wife to take the children and flee to her sister's home in Chicago. Each time she left, he promised he would change, and she returned. Each year, it seemed that this problem grew worse, and she unhappily revealed to a confidant when talking about her husband that he was "one of the best of men when sober, and the worst when drunk." Finally, on Sunday, January 11, 1880, she realized that things were not going to change and decided to permanently separate from her husband. She scanned the want ads in a Chicago newspaper, and finding a suitable opening, she wrote to her sister letting her know she was ready to leave Milwaukee, and her marriage, behind.

Wilkinson arrived home at about 9:00 p.m. that night. His children and a boarder were asleep. He had been to an area tavern with some men of the band who later claimed that they did not see him drink that night. It is unknown what transpired that night between the unhappy couple, but it is assumed that Maggie let her husband know she and the girls were leaving for good. Shortly after 9:00 p.m., a sound that resembled a gunshot was heard by a nurse and a few patients in the nearby hospital on the grounds. Just a few minutes later, the sound was heard again, and then a silence fell over the little cottage and surrounding field.

Sometime in the night, the thirteen-year-old boarder whose father was a patient at the hospital awoke and saw Mr. Wilkinson lying in the threshold of his bedroom doorway. The boy assumed the bandleader was overcome by whiskey and returned to his bed. He awoke again in the very early hours of the morning, hearing the baby crying. When the unattended infant continued to wail, he left his bed to discover both Mr. and Mrs. Wilkinson sprawled on the floor, the soles of their shoes facing each other. As he assessed the scene, it became horrifyingly clear to him that the husband and wife were dead. Clotting blood matted Maggie's long dark hair, and before the young boarder could look away, he realized that pieces of brain and gore were revealed on her right temple. The frightened boy took a quick look at Wilkinson and saw a pool of blood that appeared to come from the left side of the man's head. The boy ran to get help, but the door was locked and he could not find the key. The hungry baby continued to cry, and the panicked boy, worried that her sisters might wake up, abandoned the hunt for the key and climbed out of the window in search for help.

Running directly to his father's hospital room, the frenzied boy reported that the Wilkinsons were dead and the young girls were still in the house. The father shared the information with some men in the band room, and the group went over to the cottage to investigate. A war veteran in the group, stating that he was accustomed to seeing grisly sights, nominated himself to crawl through the window to investigate. Upon entry, he saw the horrible scene for himself. He immediately took the crying infant from her crib and passed her out the window. He returned to the window with the two still sleeping toddlers and passed them through the window as well. With the children safely removed from the gory display, the men forced their way into the locked cottage to view the dead couple.

The pale morning light streaming in from the open window illuminated the aftermath of the tragedy. The bodies lay sprawled on the floor, so close that the heels of their shoes nearly touched—each dead by a single gunshot wound to the head. The gun was near the bandleader's open hand, and his wife had one hand placed across her chest, bloodied from the single bullet hole that pierced her forefinger, telling of the woman's final, fruitless act of self-defense. Their time on earth was now over, but the effects of that night would continue to linger well into the future.

The cottages are now gone, but that area of the grounds, so near the hospital, still holds the memory of that terrible night when an angry man took vengeance on his wife and three little girls became orphans. Those walking in the area feel a sense of foreboding and fear wash over them. Some who are particularly sensitive feel a very sudden, intense headache come on, often described as a sharp pain to the temple. These effects are said to slowly disappear as those who experience them get farther from the location of this tragic murder and suicide.

The Devoted Wife: 21st Street and Kilbourn Avenue

When Ann Sidebotham met Henry Thwaits, she knew that she'd met the man she was going to marry. Ann's family was part of a group known as the "Old Settlers." Industrious and well respected, Ann's father, John, came to Milwaukee as a penniless English immigrant. Through hard work and legendary frugality, he built his businesses and obtained properties. Despite their comfortable circumstances, life was not easy for the Sidebotham children. Their father was a self-made man and required the same of his offspring; the young Sidebothams needed to make their own way in the world.

Ann likely thought she had made a good choice in Henry. The son of a former alderman, Henry had a formal education and a father who offered to help him start a business. Henry was drawn to the trades, opting to become a carpenter. He was skilled and well paid for his superior work. When the young sweethearts approached the elder Sidebotham with their plans to wed, he was anything but supportive. John's objections to the match remained a mystery, even to his closest friends, but he made his displeasure well known. In defiance of her father's opposition, Ann and Henry wed on September 6, 1874.

The marriage caused a rift between the daughter and father. John would not speak to the couple, but his disapproval began to soften after the birth of their first child. The couple lived on Cedar Street in a home the senior Thwait helped the couple purchase. As time went on, John Sidebotham warmed to the union, even having Henry participate in some of his business about town. After a bitter estrangement, it seemed that the father and son-in-law began to feel affection for each other.

By July of 1876, the family relationship appeared to be harmonious. One afternoon, the Thwait family joined the widower Sidebotham for a meal. After the table was cleared, John and Henry left together to check on a project on one of John's properties. Ann and the baby would wait at her father's house until the men returned, and then her husband would escort her home. As the hour grew late, Ann began to worry; why hadn't the men returned? The hours dragged on, and she sensed that something was awry and decided to take matters into her own hands.

Unescorted, she made her way to her home on Cedar Street but was unable to enter, as the door was locked and she did not have a key. She was overcome with the awful feeling that someone inside was desperately ill and needed immediate help. Going to her neighbor for assistance in entering the locked home, the woman also immediately sensed that someone inside the

Vintage photograph of an unknown Wisconsin family taken at the Hinderman Studio. *Author's collection*.

home required aid. Both women's intuition told them that they needed to get into that house. As their concern grew, Ann called on her brother and Henry's father, William, to help her enter the house. She grew increasingly frantic as she now felt certain that her beloved Henry was inside and in desperate need of her help.

When her father-in-law and brother arrived, they entered the home through a window and began searching the home. Henry was nowhere to be found, and nothing appeared to be out of place. They did notice two glasses of lemonade on the kitchen table and that the trapdoor in the kitchen, which opened to the cellar, was ajar. The men traveled slowly down the cellar steps, their eyes unaccustomed to the blackness of the below-ground lair. At first, it appeared that nothing was amiss, but a heavy metallic odor hung in the air and made the men look a bit more carefully around the unlit room. As they made their way to the corner of the cellar, they could feel what seemed like a sludge between their boots and the room's dirt floor. After a few moments, the men discovered that they were standing in a scene of horror. As their eyes adjusted to the darkness, they could see the body of John Sidebotham, dead—his head and body partially concealed by a steel tub in the darkest corner of the room. Soon they realized that the sticky soil beneath their feet was John's blood and gore seeping into the cellar floor. John Sidebotham had been shot in the head and left to bleed to death in his daughter's home.

The inquest into Sidebotham's death was swift, as very few people believed anyone but Henry Thwaits was to blame. The motive for the murder puzzled those close to the men. The pair seemed to be getting along well. Robbery was dismissed as an option—while it was known that Sidebotham was a wealthy man, all who knew him reported that he never carried any money on his person. Those who knew the murdered man best suggested that John had likely been murdered because of his famously stingy ways. It was assumed that the men fought over Sidebotham's unwillingness to financially help the couple and that John died because of it.

THE DEMON DRINK CLAIMS ANOTHER: THE 1000 BLOCK OF SOUTH 5TH STREET

To say the marriage of Louis and Miria Fetke was a tumultuous one is an understatement. It seems as if the man was forever in trouble, and his wife was powerless to influence his behavior. Since the couple wed, there had been a series of dustups, scandals and public scenes, but in August 1870, things could not have looked worse for the pair. They were convicted of "keeping a house of ill fame." Miria was mortified; their names were in the paper, and they were on their way to the House of Correction. She was entirely innocent of the charges, but her protests fell on deaf ears. She and her husband had been convicted due to eyewitness testimony, and the judge would not entertain the couple's denials. The pair were bound for prison.

Louis had gotten them into fixes before, as he was often running from creditors, making dishonest business deals and was involved in more than his fair share of drunken brawls, but this time was different. It looked like they had reached the end of the line, and her husband, who had been little more than an anchor weighing her down for most of their marriage, had finally dragged her down with him. The Fetkes both knew they were convicted on false testimony presented by an enemy of Louis's. The man was a dishonest drunk, but he was not a pimp, and his wife was involved in none of his dirty dealings. The couple could do nothing but let the wheels of justice turn.

Eventually, the truth was discovered and the conviction overturned. Louis Fetke saw this as a sign, an opportunity to turn over a new leaf. With some prodding, Miria agreed to begin anew with him. Together, they opened a bakery on South 5th Street, near St. Stephan's Lutheran Church. Things started well, and the bakery began to attract business from nearby bars and taverns. The couple could pay their bills, Louis was staying sober and Miria remembered the things that had made her fall in love with her husband. Soon, Miria was pregnant.

The bakery was financially successful, and Louis began the habit of stopping at each of the bars and taverns he sold to when delivering this goods. Before long, he was having a nip or two at a few favored establishments. This snowballed quickly, and soon Louis spent most of his days stupefied with drink. When the baby was born, Louis tried to stop drinking, but the onset of delirium tremens drove him back to the bottle. Miria was beside herself—she had a business to run and a baby to raise, and she needed Louis to get sober. She was certain that if he didn't, he would soon end up dead or institutionalized.

With nowhere else to turn, Miria decided to have him placed under guardianship. This would force him to dry out and prevent him from destroying the business she was working hard to keep afloat. In front of their most trusted employee, Miria quietly explained to Louis her plan to save him from drinking himself to death. As she spoke, she cradled their newborn baby in her arms, hoping Louis could see that this would be best for all of them. Upon hearing of her plan, Louis flew into a rage. He howled his opposition to the proposal and refused to cooperate. Defeated, she turned from him, still rocking baby in her arms and looking out the window to the street below, wondering what was to become of them. Lost in thought, she did not realize that Louis was approaching her from behind, axe in hand and his eyes filled with rage.

Before she realized he was there, Louis raised the axe high above his head and struck his wife in the skull. The blade penetrated the bone, cracking the skull in two. Miria collapsed to the ground, still holding the infant, and the blood-splattered bakery employee who witnessed the murder quickly fled, fearing he might be next. When the police arrived at the scene, the baby was alive and curled under her dead mother's body, and Louis, covered in the blood of his wife, fought with the officers so fiercely that they needed additional men to help detain him.

Eventually, Fetke was sentenced to life imprisonment, and the baby was adopted by one of the jailers and his wife. The bakery was sold, and life

Vintage photograph of a Milwaukeean. *Author's collection.*

continued along the Walker's Point street, but Miria's energy remains. Sensitives passing her former home and business claim to feel her presence. They sense her in a number of ways, including a sudden headache when they approach the area and an overwhelming sense of panic, accompanied by a rapidly beating heart. It is not hard to believe that a woman so swiftly taken from this world through such a violent act may have difficulty finding her way into the next realm.

The Secret that Wouldn't Stay Hidden: Riverwalk Near Menomonee and Milwaukee Rivers Confluence

Third Ward residents taking quiet walks along the Riverwalk sometimes hear the distant sounds of a child wailing. The baby's screams, although muffled, can be heard over the lapping water and the passing of cars. Confused pedestrians, their eyes scanning the water for the source of the tears, eventually walk away, assuming that the weeping is coming from a nearby building. In truth, the source of the mournful sound is both closer and farther than they realize.

Alba Dennett and his paramour, Miss Caine, had a problem in 1876, and the problem was growing bigger every month. Caine, a Prairie du Sac schoolteacher, was pregnant and unmarried, and Dennett wasn't ready to marry her. The two were terrified of the shame the birth of an illegitimate baby would cause for them and their families. After a number of panic-filled months, the couple decided to conceal the pregnancy. When their baby boy was finally born, Alba whisked the baby out of town, sending it to Milwaukee to be housed by a woman who was willing to care for the baby, and protect their secret, for two dollars per week.

The couple breathed a sigh of relief and resumed their lives as if nothing had happened; the new mother continued teaching, and the father resumed his work toward a law degree. Months passed, and no one learned of their shame. The young woman worked on plans to get the baby back into their lives in a way that would not raise the eyebrows of their families. Privately, Dennett was less interested in this plan. Very soon he would be a lawyer; he did not want any part of this carefully hidden secret to mar what he expected to be his promising future. He knew that he needed to act to preserve all he was working hard to accomplish.

One afternoon, Dennett left Madison, where he was attending school, and made his way to the Schlitz Park neighborhood where his infant son was being boarded. When reunited with his son, Dennett saw that the baby was plump and jolly. He was a favorite of his caretaker and was well loved. The woman had such fondness for him that she offered to keep him free of charge when the father told her he was taking the baby to board in another home. Dennett declined the woman's offer and left with the swaddled infant cradled in his left arm, as well as a newly acquired canvas bag that contained a few bricks on his right arm.

Vintage photograph of an infant taken at a Burlington, Wisconsin studio. *Author's collection.*

The boy was not seen again until weeks later, when a bag got stuck on the propeller of a tugboat on the Menomonee River. The bag concealed a grisly discovery: the body of the young baby weighed down by bricks, which were meant to keep him hidden from the world forever. The murdered infant was identified by his former caretaker; she identified the baby's clothes, as his face was no longer recognizable as that of the little one she had doted on months before. It took the police very little time to find Alba Dennett, and he soon confessed to the killing of his son.

The father was quickly convicted, but the infant received little justice. Dennett requested his arrest be postponed so he could take his exams but was denied. He later escaped from prison, never to be seen again. Now that little boy, whose name history has forgotten, still cries to be protected from a man who should have loved him more than all others.

CREAM CITY CALAMITIES

THE TRAGEDIES THAT CREATE HAUNTED HISTORY

Established in 1846, the great lakeside city of Milwaukee has experienced many misfortunes. The city has known catastrophic fires, a number of shipwrecks, crippling economic downturns, famously harsh weather and countless other hardships, but Milwaukee and its people always persevere. This collection of stories highlights times in Milwaukee's history when a tragedy affected many city residents. The tales had a powerful impact on the way Milwaukee was shaped, and the ripples of those terrible events are still felt to this day.

THE INTUITION OF DR. JOHN GARNER: 801 NORTH CASS STREET

Built in 1874, the building at 801–805 North Cass was originally located on 788 North Jefferson Street and then purchased and moved in 1895 by Bridget Hutchinson. The structure was probably a steal considering its history.

The home was once the residence of prominent physician Dr. John Garner. On March 2, 1876, Dr. Garner had been troubled by a peculiar feeling all day. He had an odd premonition that he was going to die. As each hour passed, the intensity of this feeling grew. So troubled was he by this sense that he spent most of his day at home, even while his family and colleagues dismissed the notion. His sense of impending doom was felt sharply at 8:25

The home was moved from 788 North Jefferson in 1895 to its current location. *Author's collection.*

p.m. He confided in his wife this seemingly irrational fear, knowing that if a patient came to him reporting these feelings, the doctor would quickly brush off these claims with a prescribed tonic and an order for bed rest.

That day, a woman named Sarah J. Willner arrived in Milwaukee from Ohio on a train shortly before 8:30 p.m. From the train station, she took a carriage to the home of Dr. Garner.

Arriving at the doctor's home, she had the carriage driver wait for her. She approached the house and rang the bell. Greeted by the Garners' young daughter, Sarah Willner requested to see him. When he arrived at the door, Willner shot him and then turned to leave the home.

Upon return to the carriage, she told the driver to take her first to a lawyer and then to the Newhall House (now the Hilton Garden Inn). When the police caught up with her, she was calmly eating a fried chicken dinner in the dining room of the once celebrated hotel.

When asked, she readily admitted to the shooting. She told the police that she had no choice but to kill Dr. Garner. She claimed that the doctor had "killed my husband, uncle, and brother and has made my life a torment. I did it in self-defense."

Investigating her outrageous claim, the police discovered a tenuous connection between Willner and Garner. They had met in Milwaukee a few years before, and he did see her husband, once, as a patient. Further investigation made it clear that she had been sending threatening letters to Dr. Garner, and he was not the only Milwaukee physician she had targeted. She was known as an "eccentric" whose behavior had become worse upon the death of her husband. At the time of the shooting, she was convinced that a group of Milwaukee physicians was trying to fill her with what she described as "medicated vapors." She had a list of doctors she intended to kill in Milwaukee; unfortunately for Dr. John Garner, his name appeared first on that list.

The resulting trial was among the most sensational in Milwaukee's history. There was no doubt that Willner had killed Garner, who died the next day due to complications from the gunshot wound he suffered. The question to debate was whether she was insane. Because many well-respected members of the Milwaukee medical community had dealings with her, they supported the assertion that she was insane and questioned why she had not been declared insane some time ago. The prosecutor vehemently believed that she was of sound mind and purely guilty. The newspapers hung on every aspect of this trial. The sensation of a shocking rarity—a female murderer—was more than the police force could handle. Eventually, the jail put a ban on people visiting Willner, as it was overrun with people coming in, hoping to evaluate her sanity for themselves.

The prosecutor prevailed, and she was declared guilty, a verdict overturned by the judge, who simply did not think the woman was sane. She spent the remaining days of her life in an insane asylum. One wonders what mysterious forces were trying to warn Dr. Garner of the dangers he faced that day and how the events of the day may have differed if he had heeded those warnings.

THE MCKENNAS' FINAL VOYAGE: LAKE MICHIGAN

It is estimated that more than 4.5 million Irish immigrated to the United States during the 1800s. Among those hopeful adventurers were Hugh McKenna and his sister. Little is known about the duo beyond their devotion to each other. Older brother Hugh was protective of his sprightly sister, and together they planned to make a go of it in their new country.

Sadly, tragedy found them in their new home. Hugh's younger sister fell ill, and despite a doctor's best efforts, she grew worse by the day. Hugh worked tirelessly, putting every penny he earned into his sister's medical care. Determined to see the twinkle reappear in the eyes of the treasured girl, he spared no expense for her care. In the end, all the efforts were in vain; the girl finally succumbed to the illness that had plagued her these many months.

Left alone and penniless, McKenna was despondent. The broke and broken man stumbled into a Buffalo, New York port looking for work during the second week of November 1901. Despite his lack of maritime experience, he was looked on with pity and offered a position on the *Syracuse*, a boat soon leaving the Lake Erie port bound for Milwaukee.

The journey started typically enough, but McKenna quickly earned the ire of the crew. The man was observed mumbling to himself and staring into space rather than focusing on the scraping and painting he'd been brought aboard to do. Soon, he was witnessed having full conversations with himself and wandering away from his work. When questioned, he always said he was off to see his sister. This bizarre behavior took a dangerous turn when McKenna scaled the mast, claiming he was following his sister up the pole. Once the man was coaxed back down to the deck, the crew realized that for the well-being of all aboard, they needed to act and seized McKenna, locking him below deck. The plan was to keep him safely detained for the remainder of the journey and discharge the Irishman in Milwaukee.

With Hugh McKenna shackled below deck, the *Syracuse* ran into a gale as it exited the Straits of Mackinac. While the ship was tossed in the waves, the crew worked to battle the angry lake. The sole focus of the men was to keep the ship dry and afloat. If they thought of McKenna at all, it was likely with relief that they did not need to worry about him while fighting the storm.

As the boat churned, McKenna was busily loosening his bonds. Convinced that his sister was in front of him and encouraging him to follow her, he strained against the shackles until they gave way. Once free, he worked to spring the lock on the door that kept him confined below deck. All the while he struggled to liberate himself, he kept his eyes on his sister, who appeared to be standing before him, flashing the smile that had brought him so much joy as they were growing up. Finally free from the restraints and the room he was held in, the man was able to follow his sister. He sprinted down the hall after her, always remaining a step or two behind her.

The brother chased his sister onto the deck of the ship, indifferent to the violent roll of the waves. Spotting McKenna at once, the men were torn; should they leave their posts and tackle the man to save him from himself but possibly jeopardize the ship? They watched in horror as McKenna raced around the deck, calling out to his sister, whom they could not see, and listened to him beg the unseen girl to slow down so he could catch up to her. He wove around the stacks, continuing the chase on the slick deck. Before he could be stopped, McKenna raced onto the roof of the deckhouse and flung himself into the lake in pursuit of his beloved sister.

As the man hit the water, the captain blew the distress signal, indicating a man overboard. The crew scanned the waves in vain, unable to spot the sailor in the rolling water. Hugh McKenna, it seemed, was truly gone. The *Syracuse* completed its journey and reported the loss when it arrived in Milwaukee. It was with more than a little relief that the crew continued back to Buffalo without the troublesome man.

A lighthouse heralding sailors to shore. *Pexels*.

McKenna's plunge into the lake should have been the end of his story, but it appears that the tale of the devoted siblings is not quite finished. As the *Syracuse* made its way across the lake, a few men were certain they caught a glimpse of the man below the waves, united with this beloved sister. As they sailed by, they saw her long red hair, billowing behind her, trailing out and encircling her brother. McKenna, submerged in the depths, appeared to have a joyful smile on his face, the siblings' arms wrapped around each other in a warm embrace. When they called others over to take a look, the two were gone.

McKenna's spirit still lingers in the murky deep. Those crossing through the Straits of Mackinac still gaze into the water, hoping to catch a glimpse of the happy siblings, connected once again beneath the rolling waves.

DUTIFUL SISTER BLANCHE:
ST. JOSEPH CENTER, 1501 SOUTH LAYTON BOULEVARD

The School Sisters of St. Francis have had a profound impact on southeastern Wisconsin. What began as an order created by German nun in 1874 in Campbellsport has grown into well-known institutions like Alverno College and Waupun Memorial Hospital. In the late 1880s, the sisters expanded their ministry with the construction of St. Joseph's Convent. Now known as the St. Joseph's Center, the prominent building sits of the corner of Greenfield and Layton Avenues. The building that stands today is not the first St. Joseph's Convent on the property.

In 1888, Mother Superior Alexia opened a convent and boarding school on the property. From the beginning, the Sisters had problems with the building that led them to sue the Chicago-based contractor for negligent construction. The order won the lawsuit, occupied the ill-constructed building and began to operate the school.

At 5:00 p.m. on March 31, the dinner hour began at St. Joseph's. There were seventy-five people in the four-story building. All the boarding school students were in the basement, eating their meal. Mother Superior was in her chambers resting, as she had been ill for some time. The infirm, eighty-six-year-old mother of parish head Father Michael was also resting in her room, and there were Sisters throughout the building performing various tasks. Sometime before 6:00 p.m., it became clear that a fire had started in the building's boiler room.

As smoke began to fill the hallways, the students were safely led out the building. By the time the women on the upper floors realized that the building was ablaze, the climbing flames prevented them from accessing the stairwells. The Mother Superior raised herself from her sickbed and warned all those she could reach of the imminent danger. The Mother tried to aid the reverend's mother, but the nun was unable to move her from her bed. Realizing that she could do nothing, the nun fled the building before she was overcome by smoke.

On the upper levels of the building, the Sisters who remained were in a dire situation. Flames made it impossible for them to exit, and they sprang toward the windows in terror, knowing that their only choice was to jump or be burned alive.

When Father Michael heard the fire alarm, he ran to the convent and was told that his mother was still trapped inside. He raced back into the building to save the ailing woman. Confused, she could not walk, but the priest managed to drag her to safety. Just after the elderly woman was pulled from the fire, the walls of the building began to crumble.

While the women in the lower levels were fleeing the building, the women hanging out of the upper windows of the flame-engulfed convent knew that they had run out of options. The collapsing walls made it impossible for the firemen to reach them. The only choice they had was to jump. Novice Rosa Minnet leaped from the window first, falling to the ground, injured but able to move herself closer to safely. Then novice Maria Weaver jumped, hitting the ground conscious but unable to move. It was later discovered that her hip had broken in the fall. The women were burned and hurt, but it appeared they would survive. Next, it was time for Sister Mary Blanka, known in the convent by the friendly nickname "Sister Blanche," to jump. The Sister, whose name had been Angela Pappe before taking her orders, hit the ground with a sickening thud. All those present knew that the woman was seriously injured before it was confirmed by the doctor.

When the fire finally burned itself out, all that remained of the former school were three charred walls. Sister Blanche had suffered multiple broken bones and extensive internal injuries from the fifty-foot fall. She was tenderly cared for until she passed into the next world on April 2. Her body was sent to the Campbellsport convent. But her spirit, it seems, remains on the grounds of St. Joseph's Convent.

By 1893, a new building had been erected on the property. Rather than operating a boarding school, the women were taking care of those in need of medical care. Life continued on the grounds, and the Sisters continued their dedicated service to those in need. The nun who lost her life continued on as well. Sister Blanche, dressed in her black habit, with her stiff white headpiece framing her face, still roams the grounds of her last earthly home. As gentle in death as she was in life, her aim is not to frighten anyone, but simply to continue to carry on her duties as a faithful member of the order.

NEWHALL HOUSE AND THE FIRE OF THE CENTURY: HILTON GARDEN INN, 611 NORTH BROADWAY

It was known as the largest and finest hotel in the West when it opened on August 26, 1857. By January 1883, some of the sparkle of the building had faded, but the Newhall House was still among the nicest places in Milwaukee. Its plush red parlors glowed in the chandelier light, and the atmosphere was always lively. There was a bit of extra excitement in the hotel the night of January 9, as internationally famous circus and vaudeville performer General Tom Thumb and his equally diminutive wife were guests in the hotel. The famous pair were headlining a show in Milwaukee that evening and were at the hotel with a number of their traveling entourage. Nearly every one of the three hundred rooms in the hotel was filled and a gentle snow had started as most of the building's occupants drifted off to sleep.

Despite its initially glittering reputation, the Newhall House had been plagued with problems. While it was known for its opulence, the string of owners who had taken control of the building could not make the business profitable. Additionally, it had a reputation as an increasingly unsafe building. The hotel was largely constructed with wood and was lit by gaslights. Local firefighters called the building a "tinder box" and warily waited for a tragedy that no one wanted but all expected. The building itself seemed to warn of what was to come, with significant fires on February 14, 1863, and January 9, 1880. The damage from the fires were notable, but no lives were lost, so repairs were made and the hotel remained open. Two fire escapes were installed on the building, each floor had a fire plug installed and there were staff on duty twenty-four hours a day. Hotel management felt that guests were safe in the hotel, regardless of the ominous predictions of the firemen.

Most people in the hotel were asleep after 3:30 a.m. on January 10. The sixty female servants in the building were sleeping on the fifth floor of the structure, and their thirty male counterparts were getting a few more hours of sleep before the start of the busy day on the sixth floor. An estimated ninety more boarders and guests filled the remaining rooms. The night clerk was at the front desk, waiting for lodgers arriving on a late train, and the night watchman was patrolling the hotel when he discovered a wisp of smoke coming from the elevator shaft. At that moment, one of the greatest tragedies in Milwaukee history began.

When the seriousness of this situation was realized, night watchman William McKinzey had the clerk run to alert the fire department at the fire box, located just steps from the hotel. The men then began their attempt to combat the fire. They quickly realized that their efforts would be worthless and began to alert the hotel guests to immediately evacuate the building. The blaze was climbing rapidly up the elevator shaft, and by the time the fire department arrived, fire was shooting out of the roof of the building.

Thick smoke filled the hallways, cutting off access to escape from the hotel rooms. Terrified guests crowded to the windows of their hotel rooms, waiting for a rescue that, for many, would never come. Obstacles presented themselves from the beginning of the rescue mission. The building was surrounded with electrical and telegraph wires that became entangled in fire ladders. The tallest ladder available, which would have easily reached the top floor of the hotel, became inoperable early in the rescue mission. The smoke and fire in the hallways made the fire escapes inaccessible to many, trapping them in rooms, some of which could not be opened from the inside. The fire raged so hotly in the building that the heat was burning the skin of those trapped inside. When flames penetrated the doors of the hotel rooms, panicked people began to flee the hotel in the only way they could: through open windows. The fear of being burned alive was stronger than the fear of the likely death that jumpers would be met with when hitting the pavement floors below.

Bodies began to pile up outside the building. Broken, bloodied jumpers were quickly moved inside area buildings. Few of the terrified jumpers survived the impact, but those who did quickly succumbed to the injuries resulting from the fall. A nightmarish scene began to unfold. The battered, burned bodies of eleven desperate servant girls lay in a heap in the alley between two building, and the horrible pile grew as the women of the fifth floor grew more desperate to escape the flames that burned their skin and scorched their lungs with every breath taken. Well-meaning but misguided onlookers called out to those clinging to the window ledges in their rooms to jump, offering to catch them in sheets and blankets. Sadly, the fabric of the makeshift safety nets was not strong enough to support the efforts, and the bodies of the jumpers tore through the material, crashing to the pavement below. The screams of terror and moans of the injured filled the air as the inferno raged on.

Some in the hotel were determined to free themselves from their rooms, quickly fashioning ropes made from sheets and propelling themselves down between the balconies. Others were lucky enough to be shepherded to safety by brave acts of those at the hellish scene. The crowd experienced a brief glimpse of hope when celebrity guest Tom Thumb and his wife were rescued from the fire. Officer O'Brien led the famous pair down a fire ladder to the street below. In more swashbuckling accounts of the story, O'Brien tucked the pair beneath one of his arms and climbed down the ladder. Other lives were spared as well. Kitty Linehan and her brother, William, were among those who saved lives that night. The siblings, both employees in the hotel, struggled to rescue as many of their coworkers as they could. William saved six lives before the heat from the fire made it impossible to continue, and his heroic sister lost her life in her efforts to ensure that the girls confined to the fifth floor made it to safety. Firefighter Herman Strauss rescued sixteen female servants from their quarters by carrying them over a walkway he constructed between the Newhall and the roof of an adjacent building using a ladder. He carried the unconscious women, overcome by smoke, across the slippery walkway over and over again until his skin was so badly burned he could not continue.

Not all deaths that night were the result of jumping from the flame-engulfed building. Some in the hotel were overcome by smoke before they woke from their sleep, dying before they were aware of the horror of the situation. More gruesomely, others were roasted by the extreme heat of the fire. Friends of a young local woman, Libbie Achellis, were forever haunted by the ghastly fate of their dear companion. As they watched in horror from the street below, they saw her kneeling, seemingly in prayer, before her open hotel window as the flames crept ever closer to the trapped girl. Helplessly, they witnessed her final moments as was fully consumed by the merciless inferno. Her screams rang in their ears as the fire raged on.

The fire took twenty-six hours before it was finally extinguished. In the end, all that was left of the once great building that stood on the corners of Broadway and Michigan Street was "a great cellar filled with ashes, broken brick and a few rods of wire road used in the elevator." The horrible reality began to set in, as a thick blanket of ice began to form over what a day before had been aflame. All of those who could be saved had been removed from the scene, and soon the street became a morgue as the effort to recover the remaining bodies from the hotel began. The hotel register burned in the fire, so it is still unknown how many perished in the flames and how many bodies still needed to be recovered from the rubble of the once fine hotel. Captain William O'Connor from the Board of Public Works headed up the corpse recovery efforts and encouraged his men to seek out areas where there was "pure white ash," which he believed was evidence of a body having been burned in the area. If the men found the tell-tale white ash without any evidence of bones or other body parts remaining, it was believed that the body was incinerated.

Reports vary on the death count of the great fire, with numbers cited between seventy-one and seventy-six souls. The bodies charred beyond recognition and without any identifying artifacts numbered forty-three. For days, the newspapers were filled with accounts of loved ones looking through rows of bodies, hoping to recover their lost family members, and then later grim descriptions of the desperate viewing charred and decaying remains hoping to find a ring or pocket watch or lock of familiar hair that would identify the remains as their own. The city mourned the loss of these unidentified causalities of the Newhall fire on January 23. There are two mass graves for those taken by the fire, one at the Catholic Calvary Cemetery and the other at the Protestant Forest Home Cemetery. This decision was made after the families of lost hotel employees requested they received the proper Catholic burial the deceased deserved. Twenty of the bodies deemed Newhall workers were laid to rest at the Calvary Cemetery, and the remaining twenty-three, believed to be guests, were interred at Forest Home Cemetery.

On that same day, the city began an inquest into the fire. Officials wanted to get to the bottom of how the fire started and what happened that escalated the fire into a tragedy so quickly. During the trial, it was concluded that the fire was a result of arson, but who committed this crime remains forever a mystery. During the investigation, it seemed as if there was plenty of blame to spread around. After intense and very public questioning of all parties, it was formally determined that the tragedy was the fault of hotel management. It was determined that the night watchman had too many duties to complete to do the job properly on his own. The failure of the night clerk to secure the hotel registry was blamed on hotel policy, as were the men's decision to try to put out the fire themselves rather than instantly evacuate the building. The inquest highlighted that the hotel did not have adequate fire measures, using as an example the brittle firehoses in the halls of the building that crumbled when the staff tried to use them. There was finally someone to blame for the tragedy, and with the blame assigned, perhaps now the city could move from the horrible events.

The grand staircase at what is now the Hilton Garden Inn. *Author's collection*.

While the location of Newhall Hotel was the site of a horrible catastrophe, it was also in the heart of rapidly growing downtown Milwaukee. The site did not remain vacant for long. By 1886, a proud stone building, known as Loyalty Block, was erected by Northwestern Mutual Life Insurance Company. In 2012, the building became a hotel. Having a hotel on the site of the worst hotel fire Milwaukee has ever experienced seems to have roused some restless spirits, and they have begun to make themselves known to the staff of the current hotel.

Employees of the current hotel tell of hearing strange sounds in empty hotel rooms and experience bathroom doors opening and closing on their own while cleaning rooms. Some have even reported instances of their hair being pulled while working in the building. While people have reported experiences all over the building, it is believed that the most active rooms in the hotel are 201 and 326. It is thought that the long-dead staff of the Newhall Hotel who lost their lives in such frightful circumstances are trying to connect with the living. Perhaps they are warning those of this realm of danger and urging them to remain prepared, as catastrophe can strike at any moment.

THE SINKING OF THE *IRONSIDES*: LAKE MICHIGAN

When *Ironsides* launched in 1864, it was among the most elegant passenger liners of its day. It dazzled with its Grand Saloon, rich wood and marble details, and delighted those aboard with its hot and cold running water. It was a true gem of the Great Lakes, moving both travelers and ore between Milwaukee and Grand Haven, Michigan. The wooden-hulled steamer was a boat of mixed reputation by 1873. It maintained its luxurious reputation with riders, but sailors and shipyard workers knew that it was a boat bound for the bottom of Lake Michigan.

The owner of *Ironsides*, Englemann Transportation Company, was a notoriously tightfisted company that habitually put profits above safety. There were few times when this practice was more obvious than with *Ironsides*. The ship leaked badly, and the problem grew worse on every journey. Men of the shipyards claimed that it needed a new hull and that the bottom of the ship was rotted out and needed replacing, but the owners, unwilling to take on the expense, patched the boat after each trip across the lake with a few replaced boards and paint. During the summer of 1873, it had begun wetting its cargo so severely that the crew would secretly unload the ship to conceal what all associated with the boat already knew: it was no longer seaworthy. Soon it became difficult to find crew to man the leaking ship at all. Rather than repairing the ship, the owners instead offered the crew higher wages to work on the vessel. The men believed it likely had a handful of voyages left in it and agreed to stay on for what they believed were its final days.

It was on this ship that Henry Valentine, a clerk with Englemann Transport, secured passage for his wife, Nettie, and young namesake son. The mother and son were scheduled to depart on the evening of September 13. Blond Henry, the beloved only child of the couple, was dressed in a brand-new blue sailor suit purchased for the journey. As the family walked from their home on Jackson Street to the boatyard, all were in high spirits. The boy's wide blue eyes sparkled with excitement as he boarded *Ironsides* that evening. The first-time sailor was abuzz with new discoveries as he explored the ship with his father. Both parents were beaming with pride over the lively boy, who garnered so much praise for his angelic looks and cheerful disposition. When the final boarding whistle sounded, Valentine reluctantly left his family on the ship and made his way back to the dock. He was unable to join them on the journey, but he felt confident that they were in good hands—after all, he had booked them on the finest passenger boat available. Valentine remained on the dock, waving at the ship as it shoved off at approximately 10:00 p.m. It was the last time he would ever see his family alive.

The mother and son rested comfortably in one of the forty-four staterooms and likely drifted off to sleep, rocked by the gentle sway of Lake Michigan's waves. During the early hours of September 14, *Ironsides* met a gale. The punishing winds forced the boat's hull to stretch and twist, rapidly multiplying the number of leaks in the bottom of the boat. Water began to rush in from the many cracks and breaks, and despite constant pumping, water was knee deep in the boat's belly by 7:00 a.m. The wind howled and the waves were relentless, eventually smashing through the gangway door. By 9:00 a.m., the engine had been flooded, leaving the boat without power. Realizing that the ship would not make it to land, the captain began the process of getting all passengers into lifeboats.

Fortunately, the ship carried enough lifeboats and preservers for all aboard. By 11:00 a.m., the ship had been cleared of passengers and crew. Separated into five lifeboats, the former occupants of *Ironsides* battled eight- to twelve-foot waves in their quest for shore. The lightweight boats were no match for the gale, and capsizing in the storm became a real fear. The boats rolled and tossed in the waves, causing some souls to be thrown from their boats and capsizing others. In the end, only two of the five boats managed to make it to shore. Among those lost in the waves were the captain, Nettie Valentine and her beloved boy, Henry. In total, twenty souls drowned in their pursuit of land.

When the storm dissipated, a few of the remaining crew guided rescue boats to the site of the sinking in the hopes of recovering survivors. Sadly, none was to be found. Nettie Valentine's body, buoyant with the aid of her still-fastened life preserver, was located that morning. After much looking, Henry was discovered, half buried in the sand. When he was freed, his appearance stunned the recovery team. His face looked placid, almost as if he were sleeping. His delicate skin was unmarred by the tragedy, and he was described by the recovery team as appearing as ethereal.

The boy and his mother were returned to Milwaukee in a pine box, with the other recovered bodies and the twenty-seven people who survived the tragedy. Mr. Valentine met the ship at the dock, scanning the crowd, hoping that the reports were wrong and eager to embrace his family. With the receipt of the pine box, his worst fears were confirmed. Nettie and young Henry were gone.

The angelic boy in the sailor suit does not rest peacefully at his Milwaukee burial site. On August 6, 2000, many think that Henry made it known that his spirit is still seeking the rescue that never came for him in 1873. During a Coast Guard festival held close to the wreckage of *Ironsides*, a thick fog rolled in, greatly reducing visibility in the area. The crew on the USCGC *Mackinaw* reported hearing sounds of a little boy calling for help in the fog. The heavy haze prevented them from seeing anything, but the boy seemed near. They called to him, trying to determine his position and implement a plan to aid him, to no avail. The persistent cries worried the men, and finally two search boats were dispatched to examine the area. The search boats were unable to locate anyone in need of help. Determined to locate the boy, the group began contacting boats that had been in the area, but the search was fruitless. No boats in the area on that day had any young passengers, and none of them had been in distress.

Taking a closer look at the area where the calls for help originated, it was discovered to be site of the *Ironsides* wreck. After no earthly source for the distress calls could be located, some are convinced that they were from young Henry, the only child on the *Ironsides* when it went down, looking for a way out of the cold water.

MILWAUKEE'S MACABRE CITY HALL: 200 EAST WELLS STREET

When City Hall was completed in 1895, it was among the tallest buildings in the country and remained Wisconsin's tallest building until 1973. The building has been a key part of Milwaukee's skyline since it was built. The unique open atrium design delighted residents and caused others to raise an eyebrow. Some superstitious Milwaukeeans were very wary of the building, particularly the design of the air shaft of the nine-floor open atrium. Many viewers of the plans noticed that the air shaft was shaped like a casket. This was even more evident when the glass was installed in the ceiling of the atrium. Those standing on the main floor of the building in the center of the atrium could look straight up and see what many thought looked like the clear outline of a coffin. To the concerned, this was a terrible omen. Within its first few decades, more and more began to believe that the building was cursed as the tragedies began to pile up in the grand building.

The notably tall building attracted those looking for a quick way to end their lives. Frances Schurmeir was not the first person to commit suicide at City Hall, but she was the first person to plunge to her death into the atrium of the busy building. Schurmeir had a difficult life. The thirty-six-year-old mother was in a burdensome second marriage to her husband, Gustav. According to him, his wife was drinking too much and he was unable to stop her. As an attempt to change his wife's behavior, the man reported his wife to the District Attorney's Office, alleging a variety of misconduct. Shortly after, Mrs. Schurmeir received a written warning from the office cautioning her to change her ways or lose custody of her beloved son from a previous marriage, fifteen-year-old Joseph.

Desperate and distraught, Frances Schurmeir made her way to the tallest building in Milwaukee on February 19, 1929. She climbed five flights of stairs and as a final, frantic act flung her body over the railing and onto the atrium floor below. She was pronounced dead as soon as medical professionals arrived on the scene. This horrible act was the first in a series that gave the casket-shaped air shaft the name "suicide well."

The next year and a half were quiet, but soon tragedy would revisit the deadly air shaft. By the summer of 1931, Leo Kraemer had built a full life for himself. The fifty-five-year-old former saloonkeeper had a wife and thirteen children. While he should have been surrounded by his large family, his growing health problems, which included rapidly developing blindness, found him a resident of the Milwaukee County Hospital for Mental Disease. Despondent, Leo believed that he was at the end of his rope. He could no longer support himself or his family, his physical condition continued to deteriorate and he was certain that he was being relocated to unpleasant accommodations on the hospital grounds. Feeling trapped by his circumstances, Kraemer made his way to City Hall on August 12, 1931.

The nearly blind man struggled to find the elevator that whisked him to the eighth floor of the building. Exiting the elevator, he was seen feeling his way along the railing that surrounds the walkway. Without warning, Leo Kraemer leaped to his death, knocking the cane from the hands of a man standing in the atrium on the main floor. His body landed with such impact that the resulting tremor brought hundreds of employees from their offices to discover the source of the commotion. They quickly discovered that the well had just claimed another life.

Then things were quiet in the building for a few years, but this peace would not last. During this time, the Great Depression had the city in a stranglehold, and there seemed no end in sight to the crushing poverty many in the city experienced. George Gazapian knew all too well how dire the situation had become. Once a successful tavern and boardinghouse owner, he was now a penniless widower living with his married daughter. On the morning of June 9, 1938, Gazapian withdrew the last $10 from a bank account that once held a balance of more than $12,000. Later that day, the West Allis resident made his way to the eighth floor of Milwaukee's City Hall. The man jumped, and the "suicide well" added another body to its tally.

Charles Darling, known as Jummy, was the next man to see City Hall's open air shaft as a way to escape life's problems. The thirty-five-year-old family man was a rarity in 1939—he was an employed man without debt. The Westside resident was a painting contractor, and his family seemed like a happy one. Dressed in his white painters' overalls, the father of two drove his work truck to City Hall the morning of February 16.

Witnesses remember seeing him walking around the lobby and other floors of the building for more than an hour. While on the eighth floor, he was spotted by a cleaning lady as he leaned over the walkway railing. She called out to him, asking him what he was doing and telling him he did not belong in the area. He replied with a stolid, "Lady, watch me, I am going to jump," and quickly flung himself over the railing to the tiled atrium floor below.

Later, his devastated family found the following note in his truck, addressed to his wife:

Esther:

This is not your fault. You are all O.K. Take care of my mother. Give her $500.

Jummy

With that, Charles Darling was gone forever, and the "suicide well" had claimed still another life.

Harry L. Kumelski was just twenty-four when he found himself opening the door to City Hall on the morning of May 3, 1939. The depressed man trudged his way up the stairs to the eighth floor. Later, an elevator operator saw the young man, who had climbed over the railing and clutched the rail with this hands as body faced the open pit. The horrified employee yelled out to him, urging him not to jump, but at that moment, he let go of the railing and plunged to the floor below.

His crumpled body landed very near forty-two-year-old Albert Pauly, who had been at City Hall delivering milk. The stunned Pauly tried to collect himself and then resumed his milk delivery route. Unfortunately, the shock proved too much for the milk man, and he collapsed about a block away from the scene of the suicide. He was taken to the hospital and later pronounced dead of a cerebral hemorrhage at 1:15 p.m. It was reported that the stress of seeing Kumelski die in such a horrible way had caused his sudden death.

Later, when the young man's body was examined for identification, the following suicide note was discovered:

> *I cannot stand it any longer. I can't figure it out myself how all this is happening to me. It is God's punishment for what I have done in my life. I just couldn't talk to tell anyone about this. Be good Catholic kids and keep your chin up. Forget about me. I'm no good. My mind is blank and my tongue is tied.*

The ominous letter had neither a salutation nor a signature. This time the "suicide well" had taken two souls.

April 1940 was a pivotal month for City Hall. By now, the term "suicide well" was widely used, and even those who didn't believe that the building was cursed because of its coffin-shaped air shaft felt that something sinister was happening in the landmark building. The city had bandied about solutions to the suicide problem, but each idea presented was determined either too impractical or too expensive. By the spring of 1940, the only real measures taken to prevent these deaths was to move potted plants into the middle of the atrium's tiled main floor to deter would-be jumpers and perhaps break the fall of those who leaped. The measure was not enough.

A vintage view of the City Hall tower. *Library of Congress.*

Unemployed husband and father of one John Alex Gorski arrived at City Hall on April 1, 1940. The despondent twenty-seven-year-old man ascended the stairs to the sixth floor of the building that morning. Without a witness, Gorski pitched his body over the railing and fell to the floor below, breaking nearly every bone in his body. As the body plummeted to the ground, it narrowly missed three people who had been in the vestibule. In the wake of the latest death, Milwaukeeans

Majestic City Hall, Wisconsin's tallest building until 1973. *Library of Congress*.

began to demand something be done to stop the ever-growing list of those taken by the "suicide well."

Just a few weeks later, Herman Theodore Rehfeld arrived at City Hall. It was just after 9:00 a.m. on April 20 when the sixty-three-year-old man entered the building. Once employed as the Columbia County undersheriff, the unmarried man was now unemployed and living with his sister and her family on 54th Street. Rehfeld slowly scaled the steps and arrived on the seventh floor at 9:30 a.m. While he looked over the railing at the lobby floor below, an employee asked him what he was doing. As a response, the man leaped to his death. The "suicide well" had taken its last victim.

Two suicides in less than a month was too much for Milwaukee to bear. The city finally decided to permanently seal the aptly named "suicide well." Shortly after, metal netting was installed to halt any further deaths. The preventative barriers remained until 1988, when they were determined to no longer be necessary.

City Hall is no longer Milwaukee's tallest building, and it is no longer a magnet for despondent residents determined to end their lives. While these horrible deaths are in the past, many believe that these unhappy souls linger in the celebrated building. Those sensitive to spirits claim to feel a heaviness in the air and detect tinges of sadness amid the ornamental splendor of the landmark. Do the spirits of those who chose death in the well remain in the building? Visit this historic building for yourself to decide if the "suicide well" kept the souls of those it claimed.

BIBLIOGRAPHY

ABC, Channel 12 News. "Haunted Landmark?" October 28, 2007. https://www.youtube.com/watch?v=XIU07hPDCao.

Anderson, Hannah. "Ghost Town." *Milwaukee Magazine*, June 2011. https://www.milwaukeemag.com/ghostTown.

Baert, Kathleen. "Yes, the Basement of Humphrey Used to Have a Morgue." Marquette Wire, March 26, 2015. https://marquettewire.org/3921049/tribune/tribune-news/yes-the-basement-of-humphrey-used-to-have-a-morgue.

Born, Jacob. "Haunted: The Ghosts of Marquette." Marquette Wire, October 30, 2012. https://marquettewire.org/3824193/tribune/tribune-news/haunted-the-ghosts-of-marquette.

Bradley, Aaron, prod. "Haunted Milwaukee." Milwaukee PBS, May 12, 2012. http://www.milwaukeepbs.org/student/student-ops-2012/watch-episodes-detail/G5mIL4FgCwA.

Breitenbucher, Cathy, and Barbara Sandler. "Flunking Murder 1." *People*, December 19, 1994. http://people.com/archive/flunking-murder-1-vol-42-no-25.

Bulgrin, Laura. "Haunting Activities of Local Ghosts Revealed." Marquette Wire, October 29, 2017. https://marquettewire.org/3756611/tribune/marquee/haunting-mg1-kw2-mn3.

Catanese, Mary. "Do Ghosts Roam the Halls of the Dousman Stagecoach Inn?" Brookfield Now, October 24, 2012. http://archive.brookfieldnow.com/news/175600121.html.

Chasco, Randal S. *Self-Guided Tour of Historic Calvary Cemetery*. Milwaukee: Archdiocese of Milwaukee, 2004. http://www.cemeteries.org/Catholic-Cemeteries/PDF1/CalvarySelfGuidedTour_Final.pdf.

Chicago Tribune. "Lloyd R. Smith Dies; Milwaukee Industrial Head." December 24, 1944, part 1.

Christensen, Willy. "Haunted Marquette." Marquette Wire, October 23, 2012. https://marquettewire.org/8028/ae/latest-issue/haunted-marquette.

Clair, Michael. "You Won't Want to Go to Sleep After Hearing These Stories from Baseball's Most Haunted Hotels." *Cut 4*, October 31, 2014. http://m.mlb.com/cutfour/2014/10/31/100209420/you-wont-want-to-go-to-sleep-after-hearing-these-stories-from-baseballs-most-haunted-hotels.

Coroner's Office of the City and County of Milwaukee, 1937. Inquest (Box No. 731, Case No. 662). Milwaukee, Wisconsin.

Demet, Maura. "Octagonal House a Many-Sided Mystery." *Milwaukee Journal*, October 29, 1984, 1.

Dretske, Diana. "Murder of Officer Petersen." Lake County, Illinois History, May 16, 2013. http://illuminating75.rssing.com/browser.php?indx=6995854&item=34.

Elmbrook Historical Society. "Dousman Stagecoach Inn Museum." 2010. http://www.elmbrookhistoricalsociety.org/dousman-stagecoach-inn.html.

Fleischmann, Bernadette, and S. Connie Halbur. *History of St. Joseph Convent, Campbellsport, 1873–1973*. School Sisters of St. Francis, Village of Campbellsport, 2005. http://campbellsport.govoffice.com/vertical/Sites/%7B247D4AC2-95B0-44CE-8C93-8CEAB868D151%7D/uploads/%7BA9732043-D46B-40E6-9C0E-104180B77E8E%7D.PDF.

Franzen, Mary. "Historic Milwaukee: Marquette's Joan of Arc Chapel." WTMJ, April 10, 2017. http://www.tmj4.com/news/local-news/historic-milwaukee-marquettes-joan-of-arc-chapel.

Gastonia Gazette. "Doc Roberts; Predicting the Future." November 6, 1977, 37.

GenDisasters—Genealogy in Tragedy, Disasters, Fires, Floods. "Milwaukee, WI Street Car through Bridge." February 1895. http://mail.gendisasters.com/wisconsin/15639/milwaukee-wi-street-car-through-bridge-feb-1895.

Godfery, Linda S. *Strange Wisconsin: More Badger State Weirdness*. Madison, WI: Trail Books, 2007.

Godfery, Linda S., and Richard D. Hendricks. *Weird Wisconsin*. New York: Sterling Publications Company, 2005.

Hintz, Charlie. "The Exorcist's Grave: The Final Resting Place of Father Walter Halloran." Cult of Weird, October 7, 2016. http://www.cultofweird.com/paranormal/exorcist-grave-milwaukee.

History of Milwaukee, Wisconsin: From Prehistoric Times to the Present Date. Vol. 1. Chicago: Western Historical Company, 1881.

Huey, Pamela. "Buddy Holly: The Tour from Hell." *Star Tribune*, February 3, 2009, Music sec. http://www.startribune.com/buddy-holly-the-tour-from-hell/38282249.

Jacobson, Brian. "A Sneak Peek of Haunted History Tours Riverside Theater." *UrbanMilwaukee*, October 27, 2011. http://urbanmilwaukee.com/2011/10/27/a-sneak-preview-of-haunted-history-tours-riverside-theater.

Jacobson, Ryan. *Ghostly Tales Wisconsin.* Cambridge, MN: Adventure Publications, 2009.

Jaques, Damien. "The White House Becomes a Clean House." OnMilwaukee, June 14, 2011. https://onmilwaukee.com/bars/articles/whitehousecelebrates120.html.

Jornlin, Allison. "Milwaukee's Little Girl Blue." Milwaukee Ghosts, January 2, 2011. https://mkeghosts.wordpress.com/2011/01/02/milwaukees-little-girl-blue.

Knopfelmacher, Delores. "History of Lake Park." Lake Park Friends. http://lakeparkfriends.org/history.

Kohler, Marie. "Indian Mounds: Wisconsin's Priceless Archaeological Treasures." *Shepherd Express*, June 15, 2011. http://shepherdexpress.com/article-15139-indian-mounds-wisconsin's-priceless-archaeological-treasures.html.

Krulos, Tea. "Milwaukee Ghost Stories: Milwaukee's Most Haunted." OnMilwaukee, October 10, 2013. https://onmilwaukee.com/buzz/articles/hauntedmilwaukeeplaces.html.

Lewis, Chad. "Ferrante's Grafton." Unexplained Research, September 28, 2004. http://www.unexplainedresearch.com/files_spectrology/grafton_ferrante.html.

———. "Tabernacle Cemetery." Unexplained Research, September 28, 2004. http://www.unexplainedresearch.com/files_spectrology/tabernacle_cemetery.html.

Ljujic, Kristina, and Heather Maricovich. "MacAllister: A History of Haunts." New Perspective, October 26, 2010. http://thedigitalnp.com/2010/10/26/macallister-history-haunts.

Loohauis-Bennett, Jackie. "Happenin' Haunts." *Milwaukee Journal Sentinel*, October 23, 2010. http://archive.jsonline.com/features/travel/105562388.html.

Markovich, Heather. "Is Carroll Building Haunted?" *The Freeman*, October 30, 2010, Local sec.

Marquette University. "St. Joan of Arc Chapel." 2015. http://www.marquette.edu/st-joan-of-arc-chapel/index.php.

Milwaukee County Historical Society. "Milwaukee County Landmarks Wauwatosa." https://milwaukeehistory.net/education/county-landmarks/wauwatosa.

Milwaukee County Parks. "Boerner Botanical Gardens Tour." http://county.milwaukee.gov/Tour10499.htm.

———. "Seven Bridges Trail." http://county.milwaukee.gov/SevenBridgesHikingTr8221.htm.

Milwaukee Daily Journal. "Burned in Their Beds." April 1, 1889.

———. "Death of Sister Blanche." April 3, 1890.

———. "Destroyed by Flames." April 1, 1890.

Milwaukee Daily Sentinel. "The Lake Disaster." September 17, 1873, 221st ed.

Milwaukee Journal. "C.F. Pfister, 68, Capitalist, Dies; Long a Leader." November 12, 1927, final ed.

———. "Ghostly Footprints Upset Quiet of Pewaukee Home." August 7, 1932.

———. "Leaps to His Death in City Hall; Falling Body Endangers Official." June, 1938, 1.

———. "Plunges to Death at City Hall; Shock Kills Bystander." May 3, 1939, 1.

———. "Scharff Is Pent Up." August 28, 1893, 1.

Milwaukee Sentinel. "City Hall Suicide Well Adds Victim." April 2, 1940, 1.

———. "Fear Caused Death Plunge in City Hall." August 13, 1931, 2.

———. "In a Fiery Grave." April 1, 1889.

———. "Leaps to Death in City Hall." February 16, 1939, 1.

———. "Murder and Suicide." April 3, 1871, 1.

———. "Officials Are Stirred Up by Latest Suicide." April 21, 1940, 2.

———. "Scharff's Black Crime." August 26, 1893, 1.

———. "She Was Insane." April 2, 1889.

———. "Woman Leaps to Death for Love of Son." February 20, 1939, 1.

Moore, Mike. "Mike Moore: Finding Haunted Places Around Here." *Racine Journal Times*, October 30, 2005. http://journaltimes.com/local/columns/mike-moore-finding-haunted-places-around-here/article_7a000fe9-f821-5c96-a72e-85da2902f711.html.

Moriarty, Judith Ann. "When Villa Terrace Was Home, Sweet Home." *Shepherd Express*, September 11, 2012, Visual Arts sec.

Muckian, Michael. "Scary Wisconsin | Ghostly Lore Part of Local Heritage." *Wisconsin Gazette*, October 19, 2012. http://www.wisconsingazette.com/

news/wisconsin/scary-wisconsin-ghostly-lore-part-of-local-heritage/article_53935348-d2d2-5b0a-b614-289511f6697b.html.

Muszynski, Lacey. "Meet Milwaukee's Ghosts: The Most Haunted Spots in Town." *Thrillist*, October 25, 2016. https://www.thrillist.com/lifestyle/milwaukee/most-haunted-places-in-milwaukee-wi.

Nagelburg, Alvin. "Nearly Complete Rainbow Spring Country Club Has Alpine Flavor." *Chicago Tribune*, November 3, 1968, 29.

Nichols, Mike. "Purported Ghosts Are Frightfully Ordinary." *Milwaukee Journal Sentinel*, October 6, 2000, Metro ed., BNews sec.

Oestreich Lurie, Nancy. "Obituaries: Stephan Francis Borhegyi 1921–1969." *American Anthropologist* 72, no. 6 (n.d.). http://onlinelibrary.wiley.com/doi/10.1525/aa.1970.72.6.02a00120/pdf.

Oleszewski, Wes. *True Tales of Ghosts & Gales*. 1st ed. Gwinn, MI: Avery Color Studios Inc., 2003.

Opsasnick, Mark. "The Exorcist's Assistant: A Look Back at the Late Father Walter Halloran." *Strange Magazine*. http://www.strangemag.com/halloran.html.

Pabst Mansion. John Eastberg, YouTube, December 18, 2012. https://www.youtube.com/watch?v=55uG4q7t1qA.

Racine Journal News. "Famous Medium Worked in Case." May 8, 1925, 1.

Racine Journal Times. "Medium Dies in Milwaukee." January 2, 1940, 7.

Rankin, J.M. "Modjeska Theater." Cinema Treasures. http://cinematreasures.org/theaters/2276.

Ritt, Lorayne. "'Curse' of Rainbow Springs Has Kept Resort's Doors Shut." *Milwaukee Journal Sentinel*, August 6, 2000, Zoned ed., Waukesha County sec.

Schjoth, Corey. "Haunted Travel: Forest Home Cemetery-Milwaukee, WI." Huffington Post, July 28, 2014. http://www.huffingtonpost.com/corey-schjoth/haunted-travel-forest-hom_b_5394631.html.

Scott, Beth, and Michael, Norman. *Haunted Wisconsin*. Minnetonka, MN: North Wood Press, 1980.

Seibel, Jacqueline, and Lisa Sink. "Fire Destroys Part of Wisconsin's Most Expensive White Elephant, the Rainbow Springs Resort." *Milwaukee Journal Sentinel*, April 17, 2002.

Sheboygan Press. "'Psychic Detective' Dies at Milwaukee Home on Tuesday." January 3, 1940, 8.

Spiekermann, Uwe. "Business and Politics: The Contested Career of Charles F. Pfister (1859 1927)." Immigrant Entrepreneurship: German-American Business Biographies, 1720 to the Present, June 8, 2016. https://www.immigrantentrepreneurship.org/entry.php?rec=274.

Sports Illustrated. "Angels' Ji-Man Choi Saw a Ghost at Milwaukee's Pfister Hotel." May 3, 2016. https://www.si.com/extra-mustard/2016/05/02/angels-ji-man-choi-ghost-pfister-hotel.

Stingl, Jim. "Blatz's Ghost a Halloween No-Show." *Milwaukee Journal,* November 1, 1990, News sec.

———. "Milwaukee Station Has Firefighters Seeing Ghosts." *Milwaukee Journal Sentinel,* October 29, 2012. http://www.firehouse.com/news/10821077/milwaukee-station-has-firefighters-seeing-ghosts.

Strub, Sherry *Milwaukee Ghosts.* Atglen, PA: Schiffer Publishing Ltd, 2008.

Swanson, Carl. "A Death at the Eagles Club." *Milwaukee Notebook,* May 22, 2015. https://milwaukeenotebook.com/2015/05/22/milwaukee-eagles-club-death.

Tanzilo, Bobby. "Urban Spelunking: Kneisler's 126-Year-Old White House Tavern." OnMilwaukee, March 23, 2017. https://onmilwaukee.com/bars/articles/urban-spelunking-kneislers-white-house.html.

———. "Urban Spelunking: The Modjeska Theater." OnMilwaukee, September 10, 2014. https://onmilwaukee.com/history/articles/modjeskaspelunk.html.

Violini, Juanita R. *Almanac of the Infamous, the Incredible and the Ignored.* Newburyport, MA: Weiser Books, 2009.

Washington Post. Obituary of Walter Halloran, March 9, 2005, B06, online edition. http://www.washingtonpost.com/wp-dyn/articles/A18767-2005Mar8.html.

Watrous, Jerome A. *Memoirs of Milwaukee County: From the Earliest Historical Times Down to the Present, Including a Genealogical and Biographical Record of Representative Families in Milwaukee County.* Vol. 2. N.p.: Western Historical Association, 1909.

Weiss, Lori. "Haunted Theater Sunset Playhouse." Filmed October 2005. YouTube, October 2008. https://www.youtube.com/watch?v=wc2ZmGkRMg0.

Wisconsin State Register. "Leaping for Life." April 5, 1890.

ABOUT THE AUTHOR

Anna Lardinois tingles the spines of Milwaukee locals and visitors through her haunted, historical walking tours known as Gothic Milwaukee. She is the creator of the self-guided walking tour collections *Walking Milwaukee: Downtown Edition* and *Walking Milwaukee: Tosa Edition*. The former English teacher is an ardent collector of stories, an avid walker and a sweet treat enthusiast. She happily resides in a historic home in Milwaukee that, at this time, does not appear to be haunted.

Visit us at
www.historypress.com